I's seen worser days dan dese when jus' a little sumpin' o' nother was good enough fer a man to get by on—when you had to cut corners to make ends meet an' keep yosef goin'. Where I used to stay I was eatin' an' sleepin' at de same time, but where I hangs my hat at an' calls home now I jus' sleeps. I eats out anywheres I takes a notion. Better times am here; dey ain't jus' 'roun' de corner—dey is right here in de middle o' de block where you can put yo' han's on 'em an' stretch yosef out 'thout wondrin' where yo' nex' meal am comin' from.

Worser Days
and Better Times

THE FOLKLORE OF THE

Worser Days

NORTH CAROLINA NEGRO

and Better Times

By J. MASON BREWER
WITH PREFACE & NOTES
BY WARREN E. ROBERTS
DRAWINGS BY R. L. TOBEN

QUADRANGLE BOOKS / CHICAGO

FOR MY WIFE

Ruth Helen

Acknowledgments

As in any work similar to *Worser Days and Better Times*, various types of assistance are needed—not only financial aid for field work and research, but the finding of persons who can furnish the material one is searching for. Those who accompany me on expeditions are important assets for collecting.

I wish to express sincere thanks to Cannon Mills of Kannapolis, Livingstone College of Salisbury, and Irvin Oestreicher of Salisbury, for furnishing the major portion of funds required to collect and assemble the material included in *Worser Days and Better Times*. Others too numerous to mention also made sizable donations which enabled me to complete the preparation of the manuscript. To W. H. (Bert) Roberts of Salisbury, who gave me some of the best tales included herein, I offer genuine appreciation and unlimited thanks.

I am grateful to the following persons who were instrumental in pointing out storytellers to me and accompanying me on my collecting tours: Grady E. Moss, Harry Neely, Charles Connor, Thomas Randall, and Rev. Elbert Fulgham, all of Salisbury; Mrs. Madeline Jones of North Wilkesboro; Joe Biggers of Durham; Rev. James L. Hunt of Asheville; and Charles Smith of Old Brinswick County, North Carolina. Thanks are also due my students at Livingstone College who made worthwhile contributions to the text.

To my wife, Ruth Helen Brewer, who accompanied me on many of my trips and made timely suggestions, I offer sincere thanks.

To Hearne Swink, vice president of Cannon Mills, Inc., and to Samuel E. Duncan, president of Livingstone College, I owe a deep debt of gratitude for constant encouragement and moral support.

Finally, I wish to express thanks to all those, many unknown to me, who had any part in providing the materials for the Folk Talk section of the book.

J.M.B.

Salisbury, North Carolina

9

Preface
Some Comments on the Collection of American Negro Folktales

The publication of Joel Chandler Harris' Uncle Remus books, between 1881 and 1905, undoubtedly inspired the impression that American Negro folktales primarily were animal stories about Bre'r Rabbit, Bre'r Fox, and their kin. As a result, collections of this sort dominated the field of Negro folklore well into the twentieth century. An excellent testimony to the existence of this impression may be found in Arthur Huff Fauset's introduction to his *Folklore from Nova Scotia*. Sponsored by Elsie Clews Parsons, Fauset went to Nova Scotia to collect folktales from the Negroes there and found, much to his surprise, that they did not tell animal tales. In his own words, which show clearly his preconceived notions of what Negro tales should be:

> What would you think of whole groups of Negroes who had never heard of Brer Rabbit? or of stories about Monkey and Baboon, Elephant, and all the other animals? Yet if you approach a Negro of Nova Scotia with the question, "Do you know the Brer Rabbit stories?" he is likely to look at you in wonderment, or even with a blank countenance, and shake his head and say, "Never heard any—what are they like?" Sometimes, after you have told him an Uncle Remus story, his face will light up a little, and he will say, "Oh, yes. I read one like that a long time ago in the Halifax Herald." After recovering from your chagrin, you say to him, "Don't you tell these stories around the fire?" He looks at you in astonishment and says, "Lord no, man, I never hears of 'em."

> These animal tales, which have become so familiar to the

general American reading public, bear very little relationship to the tales collected by J. Mason Brewer in North Carolina. A number of folklorists working in the more recent decades of the twentieth century found new kinds of folktales which earlier collectors either did not find or tended to ignore because of their concentration upon animal stories. Of these collectors, the earliest was Elsie Clews Parsons who collected Negro tales in Guildford County, North Carolina, and in other states as well, in 1917. In later years she also collected in other parts of the country and in the Caribbean.[1] That Parsons valued most highly the animal tales which she recorded is shown by the fact that she nearly always placed the animal tales at the beginning of her collections. At the same time she did collect and print Negro tales of all kinds. The comparative notes which she assembled for her tales and which led her to make several comparative studies [2] are especially valuable in understanding the relationships between the American Negro folktales and those of Africa and the rest of the United States. Parsons was also responsible for encouraging and supporting Arthur Huff Fauset in his collecting work, as previously noted. His major collecting was done in Nova Scotia among the Negro colonies there, but he also made smaller collections in three Southern states and in Philadelphia.[3] While it is true that he had a preconceived notion that Negro tales should be animal tales, and went out searching for tales which would fit his preconceptions, he also collected and published tales of many different kinds and thus helped to destroy the stereotype of the animal tale.

Zora Neale Hurston, thanks to her personal acquaintance

---

1. See the Bibliography at the end of this Preface.
2. See for example her study of "The Flight up the Tree" in *Zeitschrift für Ethnologie*, LIV (1922), 1-29.
3. See the Bibliography.

with Southern Negro life, knew that Negroes told tales of many kinds and that the animal tale was not the most important in their repertoire. She was able to collect a large number of tales of many kinds and present them in a realistic-sounding setting in *Mules and Men* (Philadelphia, 1935). Unfortunately, Hurston strikes a definite false note in the book by exaggerating the realism of the setting. For instance, she presents a group of men walking across fields and through forests, telling tales to her as they go, so that it would have been physically impossible for her to record the stories in any way. Either she recorded the tales at some other time and later placed them in this setting, or she actually heard the stories in this setting and later re-created the stories from memory only.

A much broader and more representative sampling of contemporary Negro folktales has been presented by Richard M. Dorson. Though some of his material has been published in articles in various folklore journals, the bulk of his collections is contained in two books, *Negro Folktales in Michigan* (Cambridge, 1956) and *Negro Tales from Pine Bluff, Arkansas, and Calvin, Michigan* (Bloomington, 1958). As the titles of these two books indicate, Dorson did a great deal of collecting among Negroes in the North. He found, however, that for the most part it was only recent immigrants from the South who had appreciable repertoires of folklore which he could record, and his collections therefore represent primarily Southern Negro folklore. Dorson has recorded many different kinds of tales and has shown the breadth and depth of the contemporary Negro folktale tradition. His collections are, moreover, models which other collectors could well emulate. They are accurate transcriptions of field recordings, so that we get the informant's own words, the name of the informant for each text, information concerning the informants and the circumstances of collecting, and excellent comparative notes for the tales which have been previously collected.

J. Mason Brewer has recorded and published previously tales from South Carolina and Texas. Although he has published tales of many kinds, he has emphasized the comic preacher anecdote,[4] the supernatural legend,[5] and "Old Marster and John" stories.[6] Examples of these genres have, of course, been published by other collectors, but thanks to Brewer we have a much more representative sampling than would otherwise be available.

This North Carolina collection presents tales of many different kinds. Comic preacher anecdotes and other comic tales dealing with religion are well represented. There are only a few "Old Marster and John" stories, of the clever slave usually outwitting his master. "Big John and Little John" and "The Intelligent Slave" are good examples. Both these stories, though given a setting in slavery times on a Southern plantation, are well known in other parts of the world besides the United States and are probably of a respectable antiquity.

A few stories remind us of the animal tales popularized by Joel Chandler Harris. "Both Were Proud" and "The Mountain Rat Who Outwitted the Cat," as well as the talking parrot stories, all have animal actors in them to whom are attributed human qualities including the power of speech. These stories, however, strike one as belonging to a more modern stratum of oral narrative than do the Uncle Remus tales. They are clearly humorous tales and have been collected

4. *The Word on the Brazos* (Austin, Texas, 1953).
5. *Dog Ghosts and Other Texas Negro Folk Tales* (Austin, Texas, 1958).
6. "John Tales," *Publications of the Texas Folklore Society,* XXXI (1946), 81-104.

only in the United States. Many of the Uncle Remus tales, on the other hand, are found in other parts of the world, a fact which indicates considerable antiquity.

A few supernatural legends, such as "The Stubborn Piano" and the story very commonly reported in the United States, "The Taxicab Driver and the Girl Ghost," are also included. The belief tale is represented by "Why I Left Georgia." Less commonly recorded from Negro informants is the tall tale of comic exaggeration. Brewer has found a few examples such as "The Woman Hurricane" and "Bob Benfield and the Bear," the second of which has been reported in several parts of the United States.

Many of the stories which Brewer presents can be called "protest tales," a term used by Dorson who suggests that "numerous traditional tales, involving the grievances of minority groups and the lower classes, might well be designated 'protest tales.'" [7] These protest tales range from brief, factual accounts of what might be actual occurrences of injustice and discrimination, like "Color Makes a Big Difference" and "The Arrest of the Two-Year-Old," to wry and ironic comments on integration, like "Who's Ready for Who?" Tales of this sort, which have not been too frequently recorded and published, are valuable in giving insight into current attitudes toward a major social issue.

A fair number of Brewer's stories do not fall under any convenient heading. Noteworthy, however, is a very modern quality, reflecting urban ways of life, which appears in many of the stories. One finds stories about taxicabs, postal clerks, automobiles, restaurants, and the like, which are far removed from the older notions of Negro folktales. Yet even among these stories with a clearly contemporary setting, one finds

---

7. Richard M. Dorson, *Negro Tales from Pine Bluff, Arkansas*, p. 108.

old familiar themes drawn from the great store of traditional narratives which are restricted to no one historical period or place but have existed for centuries in many parts of the world. The most striking juxtaposition of old and new may be seen in the story entitled "Race Betting." The first deals with the wager as to who can throw highest, a story usually told about how a weak but clever man overcomes a powerful but stupid ogre of some sort—but here told of a chauffeur and his boss. Although there are some adaptations here to a contemporary American setting, the basic episode clearly belongs to the old and widely known story. The second episode in "Race Betting," however, involving as it does a wager on the number of Cadillacs driven by Negroes and the funeral of Daddy Grace, must have originated in fairly recent times. Such a mixture of old and new is fairly common in folktales and adds to their endless variety. All in all, Brewer has assembled a collection of contemporary folktales which represents a broad sampling of various kinds of tales and which gives a good picture of contemporary storytelling preferences and repertoires.

A word remains to be said about the annotations which I have provided for the folktales in this collection. First of all, I have made extensive use of the references previously assembled by Ernest W. Baughman and Richard M. Dorson. To both these scholars I am deeply grateful. In citing parallels for the individual tales I have not tried to be exhaustive, especially when many other versions have been recorded. Generally speaking, I have concentrated on American Negro parallels, especially those collected in North Carolina and adjacent areas. In the use of the standard tools for folktale annotations, namely the Type and Motif-Indexes,[8] I have

---

8. See the Bibliography under Thompson.

cited type numbers wherever they apply, but I have given motif numbers only where the story could be fitted under an already existing motif; I have not tried to create new numbers. In assembling these references, I have had two purposes: to increase the usefulness of the collection for students of folklore and to give some indication of the place these tales have in the overall picture of the Negro folktale tradition.

WARREN E. ROBERTS

The Folklore Institute
Indiana University

BIBLIOGRAPHY

Note: For motifs see Thompson (*Motif-Index*) and Baughman. For types see Thompson (*Types of the Folktale*).

A. M. Bacon and E. C. Parsons, "Folk-lore from Elizabeth City County, Virginia," *Journal of American Folklore,* XXXV (1922), 250-327.

Ernest W. Baughman, "A Comparative Study of the Folktales of England and North America," Ph.D. dissertation, Indiana University, 1953.

B. A. Botkin, ed., *A Treasury of Southern Folklore,* New York, 1949.

J. Mason Brewer, "Juneteenth," in *Tone the Bell Easy,* ed. J. F. Dobie, *Publications of the Texas Folklore Society,* X (1932), 9-54.

————, *The Word on the Brazos,* Austin, Texas, 1953.

Richard M. Dorson, *Negro Folktales in Michigan,* Cambridge, 1956.

————, *Negro Tales from Pine Bluff, Arkansas, and Calvin, Michigan,* Indiana University Folklore Series No. 12, Bloomington, 1958.

————, "Negro Tales of Mary Richardson," *Midwest Folklore*, VI (1956), 5-26.

A. W. Eddins, "Anecdotes from the Brazos Bottoms," *Publications of the Texas Folklore Society*, XIII (1937), 86-105.

A. H. Fauset, "Folklore from Nova Scotia," *Memoirs of the American Folklore Society*, XXIV (1931).

————, "Negro Folk Tales from the South," *Journal of American Folklore*, XL (1927), 213-303.

————, "Tales and Riddles Collected in Philadelphia," *Journal of American Folklore*, XLI (1928), 529-557.

L. Hughes and A. Bontemps, *The Book of Negro Folklore*, New York, 1958.

Z. N. Hurston, *Mules and Men*, Philadelphia, 1935.

E. C. Parsons, "Folk-Lore of the Sea Islands, South Carolina," *Memoirs of the American Folklore Society*, XVI (1923).

————, "Folk-Tales Collected at Miami, Florida," *Journal of American Folklore*, XXX (1917), 222-227.

————, "Tales from Guildford County, North Carolina," *Journal of American Folklore*, XXX (1917), 168-200.

South Carolina Folk Tales, Compiled by Workers of the Writers' Program of the Work Projects Administration in the State of South Carolina, Columbia, South Carolina, 1941.

Stith Thompson, *Motif-Index of Folk-Literature*, 2nd ed., Bloomington and Copenhagen, 1955-1958.

————, *The Types of the Folktale*, 2nd rev. ed., FFC 184, Helsinki, 1961.

Contents

Introduction

Since the hundredth anniversary of Negro emancipation in America has recently passed, it seems appropriate to investigate what Negroes in various sections of the post-bellum South are now thinking, to record and publish what is on their minds and in their hearts. The folklore of any nation or race is the surest key to its thinking, for folk materials offer a true and unbiased picture of the ways in which a given people in a special locality think and act. Since the folkways influencing slave life and its survival in the South vary in nature and composition, Negro lore in each state of the former Confederacy should be treated separately.

Worser Days and Better Times considers the Negro folk materials of North Carolina. In the living tradition of the North Carolina Negro are the vestiges of the slave tradition and folk products resulting from the dominant forces in his new existence as a freedman. Both the inter- and intra-cultural aspects of his life are revealed. Many indigenous characteristics consistently manifest themselves in the wealth of material I have gathered in more than six thousand miles of travel which took me into practically every county and township of North Carolina, where I talked with Negroes of all ages.

Perhaps the most noticeable characteristic of the North Carolina Negro is his attitude of superiority. He feels himself superior to Negroes dwelling in states south of North Carolina on the Atlantic Coast—especially South Carolina and Georgia—and praises the intelligence and courage of fellow North Carolina Negroes at home or abroad.

Side by side with this trait is the absorbing desire of the

North Carolina Negro to go to New York City to live. It is the greatest city in the world to him, despite the fact that he knows and tells many tales about North Carolina Negroes who have migrated to New York and failed to succeed.

Unlike Negro folklore in other Southern states, tales about preachers, church members, and church officers are not abundant in North Carolina. Negroes there are apparently very serious about their religion and their religious leaders. They are critical of their ministers: rather than poke fun at them they are more inclined to seriously reprimand them.

North Carolina Negroes are great family people. Family relationships are closely knit, and there are many instances of first-, second-, third-, and fourth-generation members living in the original homestead, clinging sentimentally to the traditions of venerable ancestors who caused the family name to be revered, honored, and respected. The annual family reunion is another manifestation of close family ties; family members refer to the "Jones-Thompson Clan," etc. A public program, a big dinner, and other festivities accompany the annual celebrations. Kith and kin from all sections of the United States return for the occasion and exchange information about their activities during the past year.

North Carolina Negroes are poor visitors but sincere, helpful, and accommodating neighbors. They have explicit trust and confidence in each other and discuss their most intimate and delicate family problems freely, as if they were public property. This may account for the absence of the neighborhood brawls and petty squabbles which occur so frequently in Negro neighborhoods in other Southern states. North Carolina Negroes also believe strongly in home ownership; to them their homes are their castles.

The North Carolina Negro is very conservative, never rushing or hurrying to do anything or to get any place. One man told me, "If you're in a hurry you'd better go someplace else, because the people here believe in taking their time." This was not an understatement, for the North Carolina Negro never makes hasty decisions or rushes into any activity. He is slow to make plans, but he is a master in executing them once they are made. This "slow and steady" quality may have developed out of adherence to the mannerisms of white North Carolinians, since history tells us that the state was once referred to as the "Rip Van Winkle State."

There is almost as much class tradition among North Carolina Negroes as there is mass tradition. Many rural communities in the state are composed entirely of Negroes whose ancestors were free—some of whom owned slaves themselves. Most of the descendants of these groups are farmers and live in their own communities where their customs are strict, well defined, and adhered to in a dogged and persistent manner.

The North Carolina Negro is still somewhat superstitious, but more *suspicious* than superstitious. This make-up is vividly reflected in an experience I had with an elderly Negro whom I encountered on a trip through the state in the summer of 1961. I was on the lookout for a wagon drawn by a mule, and a short distance ahead on the road I saw an old man parked by the roadside in a small wagon with a mule hitched to it. I told my companion to stop the car when we reached the spot where the old man, who seemed to be in a meditative mood, was seated. I then walked over, introduced myself, and asked the old man if he would mind my taking a picture of him and his mule to be used in a book I was writing. He proceeded to revile me and to tell me that all "educated niggers" like me ought to be dead. He added that Booker T. Washington should never have been born—nor President Kennedy, nor any other prominent person. He ended his tirade by saying that he had two children who had finished college and that they were the biggest fools in the whole family. When he had finished bawling me out, I thanked him courteously for his time, got back in our car, and drove off.

A similar incident occurred when I called on a prominent retired businessman upon the invitation of his daughter, who thought he had some information that would fit the plan of *Worser Days and Better Times*. I met the old gentleman and told him that he had been recommended to me as a possible source of information vital to the success of the book I was writing. He looked at me in a disdainful manner and in no uncertain terms told me that he was writing a book himself. He was going to put everything he knew in his own book, he said, so I might as well go someplace else and get my information, because he wasn't "going to tell me nothing."

The North Carolina Negro is punctual on the job but negligent about attending public meetings on time. In one North Carolina town where there is a Negro college, some of its students began attending a white church in the community, without incident and without protest from the minister or the congregation. After the students had attended the church for several Sundays, the president of the college had a telephone call from the pastor of the church, with whom he was well acquainted. The minister said, "Please tell your students that we are glad to have them worship with us, but add that if they see fit to attend our services we would appreciate it if they would get to the church on time."

It might be well, in conclusion, to say a word about the pattern of *Worser Days and Better Times*. In my previous folklore collections the contents have been rewritten and restyled by me. They have been "something of others" and "mostly of me." In this book the styles and materials are "mostly of others" and "something of me." In order to preserve the peculiar folk flavor of the individual offerings, I thought it wise to keep editorial interference at long range.

Another deviation from my usual procedure is the anthological structure of the book. Heretofore I have limited my reporting to the folk narrative, but here I have combined the folktale with other interesting specimens of oral literature, history, and tradition.

I think it advisable, also, to explain why no informants are listed in the work. Since most of the material was recorded without the knowledge of the contributors, I saw no reason to list some of them if I could not list them all. Most of the items included in the book were gathered while I was a passenger on a bus or train, or seated in cafés or drugstores or barber shops, or standing on street corners. The only exceptions are the autograph album rhymes. I believe a more authentic and natural product can be obtained when the informant is unaware that what he says is being collected.

1

Folktales and Anecdotes

*That's all the girl lives next door to me does
is tell tales; she talks real loud, too.*

North Carolina Negroes are generally honest, pious, and dependable by inheritance. Most of their early slave masters were English and Scottish farmers who, in the main, had a high regard for strict adherence to basic Christian living. The more devout slave masters forebade overseers from swearing at or before slaves, for if it was disrespectful for the slave to swear at his overseer, it was equally disrespectful for the overseer to swear before his Maker.

Negroes imitated their pious masters and took their religion seriously. They objected to white ministers who, while preaching at the same time to slaves and white plantation families, faced the white worshipers and turned their backs to the black congregation. The Negroes complained about services in buildings so small that only white churchgoers could be seated inside.

Religion is no laughing matter to the North Carolina Negro; it is rather a sacred and devout obligation. Yet several religious tales and anecdotes have acquired the status of group property and may be classified as traditional Negro narratives. They are still told among non-churchgoers—and a few churchgoers.

Many other North Carolina Negro tales highlight the

stupidity and ignorance of South Carolina and Georgia Negroes, and the courage and intelligence of North Carolina Negroes. Other favorite anecdotes belong to a type I call the "migrant tale," commenting on the sad plight of North Carolina Negroes who leave the state and go to New York City ("up the road" or "up the country") to live.

The North Carolina Negro's feeling of superiority does not limit itself to the members of his own race who dwell in areas south of North Carolina. He also thinks himself better and more intelligent than mountain whites and poor "city whites," and takes great delight in spinning yarns about their stupidity, imitativeness, and other bad qualities he claims they possess.

The few tales that North Carolina Negroes tell about Indians, although comical in nature, do not always ridicule the Indian's native intelligence or wisdom. Many North Carolina Negroes number Indians, especially Cherokees, among their ancestors, and it appears from his storytelling that the Negro regards the Indian as a victim of discriminatory practices like himself. In Siler City, North Carolina, there are separate accommodations at movie theaters for whites, Negroes, and Indians—the latter two groups being assigned separate balcony sections. There are also separate Indian schools operated by the state, just as there are separate Negro schools.

There are a few tales of slave days still being told by direct descendants of ex-slaves; there are some narratives about hurricanes; and now and then a ghost story rears its ghastly head among the folktales still remaining in the living tradition of the North Carolina Negro. The once-popular animal tale about Bre'r Rabbit and other creatures has almost reached the point of extinction and appears only at scattered intervals. The old, "other worldly" theory that influenced Negro thinking during the slave era, when the animal tale thrived, has been replaced by what may be called "reality thinking": the Negro faces life situations and problems realistically. Consequently, his comments on his existence, in the form of folk narratives, describe real people and their experiences.

Tales about Religion and Church

THE PARROT WHO ADVERTISED TOO MUCH *

Speakin' o' one thing an' talkin' 'bout another, dey was a colored fellow in Greensboro what come into some money an' thought he'd open him up a liquor store. So he rents him a place, but dey's 'bout five mo' liquor stores in de same block, an' since dey been dere long 'fo' he start his business, dey gets mos' all de trade. Dis here make de man do a whole lots of worryation, 'cause he done sunk all his money in de business, and it ain't payin' off. So he study, an' he study, an' he study, an' finely he come up wid what he think de right answer to de problem. He 'cide to get him a parrot an' put de parrot outen front of de store an' learn him to holler, "Liquor store, liquor store, liquor store." So he do just dat, an' put de parrot outen front of de store in he cage dat next comin' Saddy mornin', hollerin', "Liquor store, liquor store."

Dis here sho pay off, 'cause 'fo' hit done come to be

---

* This story, which can be referred to Motif B211.3.4. "Speaking parrot," is quite common in a slightly different form in modern urban tradition. Neil Rosenberg, is an unpublished MA thesis, "An Annotated Collection of Parrot Jokes" (Indiana University, 1964), pp. 53-54, gives a version he recorded and cites five other versions in the Indiana University Folklore Archives recorded by college students, together with another version from a work devoted to obscene jokes, entitled *Anecdota Americana*, which was published in 1934. In all seven of these versions, however, the parrot which recognizes customers in church is from a house of ill repute rather than from a liquor store.

33

twelve o'clock de man done tuck in five hunnud dollars, an' have to order some more liquor to last him thu dat day. From dat time on he have mos' de trade in dat block, 'cause de peoples lacks to hear de parrot out dere squallin' out, "Liquor store, liquor store."

De man thinks so much o' de parrot for what he done did for him till he takes him to church wid him one Sunday mornin'. Dey gets to de church-house a lil early, so dey takes a seat in de back of de church-house where dey can see all de peoples what comes in. De old parrot was settin' on de man's shoulder, an' ever time somebody'd come in he'd look back. Soon everbody he seed come in done been to buy whiskey from de liquor store. So all of a sudden de old parrot started yellin', "Liquor store, liquor store, liquor store."

"Shut up," say de man, but de parrot don't pay him no heed; he just keep on hollerin', "Liquor store, liquor store, liquor store."

"Listen here," say de man, didn't you hear me tell you to shut up; dis here's a church-house." Den de parrot look up at him kinda pitiful like an' say, "Same crowd, same crowd, same crowd."

THE CABARRUS COUNTY BOY WHO TOLD THE CHURCH WHAT TO DO *

Sittin' 'roun' listenin' to old folks you can learn a lots, but you can learn a lots by goin' up de road to New York, likewise.

---

* I know of no exact parallels to this story, though it is similar to another story in which the word "cuspidor" is thought to refer to an elective office. The chairman of a meeting has received nominations for various offices. He is chewing tobacco and finally says,

One time dere was a boy what left home in Cabarrus County, went up to New York, an' comed to be in good shape. When he done come to be in good shape, an' have him a little money on de side, he makes his way back to see his mama an' papa what done been his standbys 'fo' he lef' home. Dey is real proud of de boy, 'cause he got a lots of fancy clothes, a bran' new car, an' some money in his pocket. So dat next comin' Sunday dey all gets ready an' goes on down to de church.

Dey gets dere a little 'fo' de services starts, so de boy shuck an' reshuck de hands of most de members what know him from a little chap, and den goes on into de church-house wid his mammy and pappy.

After de sermon am over de preacher gets up an' say, "Now brothers an' sisters, I has sumpin' dat got to be 'cided on right here dis mornin'. It's 'bout de money we done raised; an' de question am, what must us get wid de money, a piano or a chandelier?"

Den one of de members what been knowin' de boy from time he was knee-high to a duck riz up an' say, "Brother pastor, we has a visitor 'mongst us dis mornin' what done been up de country an done come to be a knowledge man.

"Now we need a cuspidor," whereupon a member leaps to his feet and shouts, "I nominate so-and-so for cuspidor." This cuspidor story is classified by Baughman as Motif J1772.22.* "Cuspidor thought to be appointive office." He cites Carl Carmer, *Listen for a Lonesome Drum* (Garden City, 1940), p. 294. It was also collected by Dorson in upper Michigan (*Bloodstoppers & Bearwalkers* [Cambridge, 1940], p. 102). Another story, perhaps even more closely related, was printed in the Louisville *Courier-Journal*, November 1, 1964, Sec. 4, p. 5. In this Kentucky story a group of church members are discussing how to spend some available money. One proposes that they buy a chandelier. Another member objects, saying that what they really need is a light fixture.

Sposin' we asks him what we ought to buy wid de money?" De pastor say dat's awright wid him; just whatsomever de membership want to do wid de money, an' whosomever dey wants to pass judgment, cause dey raised it. So de boy gets up, pokes his chest way out, rams his han's way down in his pockets an' say, "Well now, I tells you. If'n I was y'all I believe I'd buy a piano wid de money, 'cause as far back as y'all is in de woods I don't believe you gonna find nobody out here can play no chandelier."

THE HYPOCRITICAL SISTER *

One Halloween night in Marion, after the party broke up, a little boy stopped by the church-house to get his mother. The boy wore a devil's suit and mask, and still had it on when he entered the church. When he opened the door everybody ran out except one old lady. She said, "Wait a minute, Mr. Devil! I have been in this church for fifty years, and believe it or not, I have been on your side all the time."

---

* Cf. Motifs J1786. "Man thought to be Devil" and K1838. "Disguise as Devil."

HOW THE PARROT BROKE UP THE CHURCH MEETING *

A preacher was running a revival, and every night he would tell the people that they were going to hell by the wagon-loads. Old boss had a parrot, so he told the parrot to go down to the church and ask who was going to bring the wagon back. The next night as the preacher made the statement the parrot said, "Who'll bring the wagon back?" Everybody ran out of the church but one old lady, so the parrot lit on her shoulder and said, "Who'll bring the wagon back?" The old lady said, "I don't know, Mr. Jesus. I'm ain't a member here, I'm just a visitor."

ONE TIME GOD DIDN'T DO RIGHT †

One time a woman moved into a new neighborhood. The first Sunday after she moved into the neighborhood one of her neighbors invited her to go to church with her. The woman thanked her neighbor for inviting her, but told her that her husband had to go back where they moved from to get some things they had left, so she didn't have nobody to leave the children with. But her neighbor said, "Oh, that

---

*Another North Carolina Negro version of this story was collected by an Indiana University folklore student, Barbara Smetzer, and given in her unpublished MA thesis, "An Annotated Collection of Negro Folktales from Harnett County, North Carolina" (1962), pp. 50-51. It was also reprinted in Hughes and Bontemps, pp. 161-162, from E. C. L. Adams, *Congaree Sketches*.

† Cf. Motifs J2495. "Religious words or exercises interpreted with absurd literalness." and J2499.5. " 'God is everywhere.' "

ain't nothin', just come on and go and leave the children in the hands of the Lord." So the woman who had just moved into the neighborhood said, "All right then, I'll go with you, so come by for me."

When Sunday mornin' rolled 'roun' the neighbor was right there for the woman, so she left her children at home and went on to church.

When they got to the church-house and went in, the preacher was prayin' his openin' prayer. He said, "Lord I know you's here wid me, you's always wid me." And when the woman who had just moved into the neighborhood heard him say this she jumped up out of her seat, and said, "Humph! You can't even trust God. I told him to stay at home wid my children, an' here He is sittin' up in church."

THE CHURCH THAT JESUS COULDN'T GET IN *

One time a man repented of his sins and went to join the church on the following Sunday. When they called for new members and extended the invitation for folks to join the church, the man who had repented of his sins walked up and told the preacher he wanted to join. The preacher looked at him and said, "Have you been redeemed?" "No," was the man's answer. "Then, I'm sorry." said the preacher. "You can't join this church now; you have to wait until you been redeemed."

The man went back to the church every Sunday for three months, but the preacher still refused to let him join it. Before the man could start the fourth month off at the

---

* This story is given in W. Pickens, *American Aesop*, reprinted in Hughes and Bontemps, pp. 158-159, and in J. J. McDonald, *Life in Old Virginia*, reprinted in Botkin, p. 100.

church he died and went up to Heaven. Upon reaching the pearly gates he told St. Peter about how the preacher at the church had treated him. So St. Peter replied, "Oh, don't worry about that. Jesus has been trying to get in that church for 1,900 years, and he ain't been able to get in it yet."

THE PREACHERS AND THE CAB DRIVER
AT THE HEAVENLY GATES

One time there was two preachers and a cab driver that died and went to Heaven at the same time. They all went up to the Pearly Gates to be judged by St. Peter. One of the preachers was the first to approach St. Peter and make his confession. He said, "I have been preaching for fifty years." But Peter did not let him in the pearly gates; he told him to step aside. Then the next preacher came forward and made his confession to St. Peter. He said, "I have been preaching for twenty-five years." But Peter told him to step aside, like he did the first preacher. Then the cab driver came up to where Peter was seated, and confessed that he had been driving a cab for fifteen years. So Peter told him to enter the pearly gates.

When the preachers saw this they asked Peter why he let the cab driver enter the pearly gates and would not allow them to enter, when the two of them together had preached a total of seventy-five years while the cab driver had only been driving a cab for fifteen years. "I let him in," replied Peter, "because he's scared the hell out of more people in that fifteen years than both of you have in seventy-five."

THE DIVIDED CHURCH

Some churches is sho hard to pastor. One of 'em dat I knows 'bout is right here in Kinston—dat is, it's 'bout ten miles out on dat ol' dirt road what runs into de main highway. Dey calls de church Mount Zion, an' as far back as I can remember ain't no preacher stayed dere more'n a month o' two. My mind reaches back forty years o' more, too, an' I ain't never seed dat church hol' a preacher ver' long at a time.

But las' year sumpin' nother happened dat make me switch my mind roun' 'bout dis church can't hold no preacher. It was long 'bout watermelon time las' summer when a new preacher come to Mount Zion to try hissef out. De first Sunday he preaches he gets along jus' fine, but de secon' Sunday he take notice dat de ver' same members what set on de right han' side o' de church sets on de right han' side o' de church de secon' Sunday, likewise, an' dat de ver' same members what set on de lef' han' side o' de church de first Sunday sets on de lef' han' side o' de church on de secon' Sunday. On de third Sunday, de fourth Sunday, an' de fifth Sunday he take notice dat dis here same thing happen, so after de services was over on de fifth Sunday he calls de head deacon o' de church an' say, "Listen here, brother deacon; I wants to ask you a question 'bout sumpin' I sees dat I doesn't like." So de deacon say, "What dat you see you don't like, brother pastor?" An' de pastor say, "I don't like it 'bout de church bein' divided—de same members settin' on de same side o' de church ever Sunday, so I wants you to tell me why dey carryin' on in dis wise."

"Well now, elder," say de deacon, "I ain't gonna tell you

nothin', 'cause dey ain't nothin' dat you o' me o' nobody else can do 'bout it." So de pastor turnt on his heels 'thout sayin' another mumblin' word, an' got in his car an' drive off.

But dat nex' comin' Sunday he gets up in de pulpit to preach 'bout brotherhood an' 'bout how church folks ought to be together 'stead of bein' separated. His sermon ain't hit bed-rock nowheres though, 'cause dat nex' Sunday all dem what been settin' on de right han' side o' de church-house comes right back an' sets on de right han' side like dey always do, an' dem what been settin' on de lef' han' side o' de church comes in an' takes dey seats on de lef' han' side, like as always.

De preacher be outdone; he don't know what to do, so after de services he tell de head deacon dat he want to have confab wid him again. He done stayed dere longer'n any preacher dey done ever have, so he know dey won't get rid of him if'n dey can help it. So he say, "Now look-a-here, brother deacon, I means business; if you don't tell me de why de same members o' dis here church sits on de right han' side ever Sunday, an' de same members sets on de lef' han' side o' de church ever Sunday, I's gonna pack up my clothes an' find me another church."

De head deacon don't want de church to lose dis preacher, so he finally give in an' say, "Well den, brother pastor, I tell you why de same ones sets on de right han' side ever Sunday, an' de same ones sets on de lef' han' side ever Sunday. Ever since I was a little fellow runnin' 'roun' in pigtails an' my mammy an' pappy brung me to church, dis here been goin' on. You see, it's like dis: dem what sets on de right han' side o' de church-house ever Sunday says, 'Dey ain't no Hell,' an' dem what sets on de lef' han' side says, 'De Hell dey ain't!' "

WHEN GOD LOST OUT *

One Sunday morning a white man got off the bus in Kannapolis and got into a taxicab driven by a white man. He asked the taxicab driver to take him to the Church of God. "I ain't heard of no church like that here in Kannapolis," said the taxi driver, "but I'll try to find it for you." So saying, the taxi driver started his car up and left the bus station. He drove first to the Lutheran Church and said, "This here church belongs to Mr. Cannon." Then he went to the Presbyterian Church and said, "This here church belongs to Mr. Cannon, too." Then he drove to the Baptist Church and said, "This here church belongs to Mr. Cannon!" He then drove on to the Methodist Church and said, "This church belongs to Mr. Cannon, too." Then he added, looking back at the visitor, rather sadly, "Mister, I don't believe God's got no churches here. All these churches belongs to Mr. Cannon."

THE ANGEL WHO WANTED TO GO TO HELL

One time dere was a ol' boy 'roun' China Grove what come to be de bes' gospel singer in dem parts. Nother thing,

---

* Kannapolis, North Carolina, was founded by James W. Cannon, textile manufacturer, founder and owner of Cannon Mills, in 1905. He continued to expand his business until his death in 1921, at which time his youngest son, Charles A. Cannon, now president of Cannon Mills, began directing the enterprise. It is Charles Cannon to whom the anecdote refers. Kannapolis is Greek for "city of looms." It is said to be the largest unincorporated city in the world, with a population of 30,000.

he lib a good Christian life, too. His name ain't nevuh been up on de signboard lack mos' all de rest o' de younguns 'roun' China Grove. Dis ol' boy, what go by de name o' Jasper, hab a good name wid de ol' peoples an' de young. All he do was go to choir practice durin' o' de week, an' to chu'ch services all day on Sunday. He ain't never yet been to no fleng-dang [dance] dat dey hab ever Saddy night, an' he ain't never been in no pool hall neither. He just stay in de house all de time an' practice singing chu'ch songs.

One Sunday night, how-be-ever, when he was drivin' his ol' car home from chu'ch, de brakes gib out, an' de car leaves de highway an' falls over in a ditch 'side de road an' kill 'im.

Nachully, he was 'mitted to de pearly gates o' Hebun, an' was one o' de choice angels. De first Saddy night he was dere, all de choice angels was settin' 'roun' God's throne lookin' at de TV program an' it happen dat ever Saddy night dey looked at a special broadcas' from Hell. Dis' ol' boy, Jasper, seed a jazz ban' playin' de blues, an' some putty gals shakin' deysef an doin' de "twist," an' de "jerk" down in Hell, so he touch God on de shoulder an' he say, "God, how 'bout lettin' me go down to Hell?" So God say dat's awright wid him, but if'n he go down to Hell he gonna hab to stay down dere an' he can't never come back to Hebun no mo'. Jasper say dat be awright wid him, so he leaves Hebun an' goes 'on down to Hell. It was 'bout nine o'clock dat night when he lef', but 'long 'bout midnight God hears somebody knockin' on de Hebunly gates, an' when he peeks over de wall to see who it is knockin' on de gates dat time o' night, he sees dis ol' boy Jasper an' say, "Look a-here, what's de matter wid you comin' back up here to Hebun? Ain't I done tol' you dat if you went down to Hell you's gonna hab to stay down dere?"

"Oh, yassuh," say Jasper, "I unnerstood dat in de first place. I jus' come back after my clothes."

THE BOY WHO PLAYED JESUS

One time a ol' boy what lived out to Pleasant Plains, in Winton Township, what belong to dat "almos'-white" bunch o' folks dey calls "Free Issues," come to learn how to play de organ an' de piana real good, so no sooner'n he done finish up in de high school he tells his mama an' papa dat he wanna go up de road an' come to know mo' 'bout how to play de organ an' de piana. But his mama an' his papa say "No"—dey ain't gonna have him lightin' out from home at no sixteen years ol'.

After dis de boy sit 'roun' de house an' won't open his mouf to his mama an' papa, but dey hol's fas' to what dey says 'bout him not goin' up de road to come to know how to play de organ an' piana better'n he do now.

Howbeevuh, one Saddy when his mama an' papa done drive into Ahoskie to git some tools for de farm, dis ol' boy packs his clothes into a bag an' goes out to de highway to catch him a ride. He gets him a ride as far as Norfolk, an' from dere he catches de train an' goes on to New York.

When he gets to New York he goes down to Harlem, an' rents him a li'l room in a basement. He got a little money dat he kin call his own, so it las' him a li'l while, but putty soon hit 'gin to give out, an' he starts lookin' for a job. But since his folks was land-ownin' farmers an' hire dey help, dis ol' boy don't know nothin' 'bout no work an' he can't fin' nothin' to do.

Dis worry him a lots, 'cause his money 'bout all gone, so one day whilst he was stannin' on de corner thinkin' 'bout he might have to go back home, a man passed him an' say, "Man, you looks like Jesus"—de ol' boy done really growed a beet-nick beard, so when de man tell him dis he hurry down to his li'l room an' look in de lookin'-glass at hisse'f, an' sho nuff, he do look like Jesus. No sooner'n he done peeked at hisse'f in de lookin'-glass he goes down to a Jew store on de corner an' buys him a long white robe. Dat nex' comin' Sunday he puts de robe on an' goes down to a big Baptist Church in Harlem, an' starts walkin' comin' down de aisle towards de pulpit, when de preacher see him an' say, "Hol' de singin' a minnit. Here comes Jesus. Let's take up a collection for him." So dey takes up $200 an' gives it to de ol' boy. Dat nex' comin' Sunday he goes down to a big Catholic Church an' goes in an' starts walkin' down de aisle wid his han's stretched out, so de priest sees him an' say, "Here comes Jesus, let's take up a collection for him." So dey takes up $200 an' gives it to him. De ol' boy say to hisse'f, "I sho got sumpin good workin' for me now." So nex' comin' Sunday de ol' boy puts on his long white robe again, an' goes down to a Jew synagogue an' starts walkin' down de aisle wid his han's stretched out. Dere was two rabbis 'ductin de services, so when dey seed de ol boy walkin' down de aisle one of 'em yells to de other one, "Go an' git de hammer an' nails quick; de fool's off de cross again."

Tales about Ministers

BOTH WERE PROUD

One time dere was a mainstay of a church down in Davie County what have twin boys. He such a good church-member till de boys 'cides dey wants to be preachers when dey grows up. So after dey done end up wid high school dey papa sends 'em off to 'nother school where dey can learn to know how to preach.

After dey done wind up dey lessons at de preacher-school dey come back home to 'liver dey first sermon. De mainstay o' de church an' his wife was proud as dey can be o' dere sons, so whilst dey was preachin' dey was sayin' "Amen" all de way through de sermons.

De way dey have it set up—one o' de boys would preach ten minutes, den de other'n would preach ten minutes. Dey preached a whole hour long off an' on, an' de whole congregation liked de way dey carried out.

After de service was over de mainstay o' de church an' his wife carries de boys on home where dey have a big dinner for 'em to smack on. 'Mongst de food was two young fryin'-size roosters what dey catched off dey yard an' kilt.

When dey done et, dey all goes out into de yard to get a li'l whiff o' cool air, 'cause hit was in de month o' August, an' a turbul hot day. De mainstay an' his wife was settin' on a old bench under a tree, an' dey two sons was settin' in some old rickety chairs underneath 'nother tree fannin' dey-sefs wid some newspapers. De mainstay o' de church say to his wife, "Ain't you proud o' our two sons what just entered de ministry?" And when he talk in dis wise, de old

46

rooster what was de pappy o' de two fryin'-size chickens de
young ministers done et for dey dinner, and what was listenin' to what de mainstay say to his wife, turn to de hen
what was de mammy o' de fryin-size roosters, an' say, "Ain't
you proud o' our two sons what just entered de ministry?"

THE PREACHING OF THE SINFUL BROTHER'S FUNERAL *

One time a man's brother died in Rowan County. He was
so wicked that none of the preachers in the community
would preach his funeral. So his brother went around into
all of the neighboring communities to see if he could find
somebody to preach the sinful brother's funeral. Finally he
succeeded in finding a raggedy and hungry preacher who had
no church, and who told him he'd preach his brother into
hell for $2.98, into purgatory for $3.98, and into heaven for
$5. So the live brother told him he'd pay him $5 to preach
the dead brother into heaven. So the man took the preacher
out to his house in his horse and buggy. When they got
there all the relatives and friends of the sinful brother were
there. So the hired preacher began to conduct the funeral
services. He preached for about thirty minutes, but just before
he reached the end of the sermon he turned to the dead
brother's brother who'd hired him, pointed his finger at
him, and said, "Well, brother, I's got him jes' one step out
of heaven now; so I tells you what I'll do—for another fifty
cents I'll preach him right on into heaven."

"I ain't gonna pay you another cent," replied the live

---

* The same tale, as collected from Philadelphia Negroes, is given
by A. H. Fauset, "Tales and Riddles Collected in Philadelphia,"
Journal of American Folklore, XLI (1928), 550.

brother, looking up at him. "If he cain't step dat other step into heaven, he can jes' go on to hell."

THE PREACHER AND THE RUNAWAY LION

One Sunday in Durham an old preacher was telling his congregation about belief and faith in prayer before the eleven o'clock services began. He had been informed just a few minutes before that a lion had broken loose from a nearby zoo, so he was telling his audience to have faith in God, and not be afraid of the lion if they should run across him on the way home after services. "If you pray hard enough," he said, "fear not, for the lion outside will not bother you." He shouted very loudly, "Fear not, for thou art with me; watch, and I will show you a way to get out. I have the faith in God that all y'all should have."

But after the services were over, before the preacher had gone more than a few yards from the church-house steps, he was met by the lion. The preacher got down on his knees and said, "Oh Lord! please hear my prayer. You saved Daniel from a lion, and I know you gonna save me from this here lion." His prayer was loud and sincere; but, all the same, he raised his head after a while to see what the lion was doing. To his surprise, he saw that the lion was also kneeling, with his paws clasped over his eyes. So he said, "Brother lion, are you praying wid me?"

The lion looked up at him and replied, "No, brother, I's sayin' my grace befo' I eat."

THE TRAVELING MINISTER *

One time there was a traveling minister. He went from place to place, spreading the gospel, but he got so tired and sleepy one day that he stopped to take a nap. It was the fall of the year, and while he was asleep some devilish little boys slipped up on him and raked some dry leaves that had fallen off the trees all around the minister. Then they set fire to the leaves. When the leaves started to burning the old minister woke up and saw the fire all round him, so he jumped up and started yelling, "I'm in hell, just as I expected."

THE PREACHER, THE DEACON AND THE FRESH AIR †

One time a preacher in the pulpit was preaching, and every now and then he would stop preaching and say:

Let's sing a little song,
Let's say a little prayer,
While I step outside
And get a breath of fresh air.

---

* In a story from a Negro colony in Nova Scotia, a minister who thinks Judgment Day has come races across a field and falls into a ditch. When he returns to consciousness, he says, "I'm in hell, just where I expected to land" (Fauset, *Nova Scotia*, XXIV, 94). Cf. also Motif J2322. "Drunken man made to believe he has been to heaven and hell."

† This story is of particular interest in that, while it is reasonably well known in Scandinavia and adjacent countries (Type 1827), this seems to be only the second time it has been recorded in the United States, in both instances from Negro informants. See Parsons, *Sea Islands, Memoirs of the American Folklore Society*, XVI, 127, for the other version.

Then he would go outside and reach under the church-house steps and get a bottle of whiskey he had hid there, and take a drink. Then he would go back in the church and start preachin' again, but pretty soon he'd stop preachin' again and repeat:

> Let's sing a little song,
> Let's say a little prayer,
> While I step outside
> And get a breath of fresh air.

Then he'd go outside again, look under the steps, and get the whiskey out, and take a drink of it.

He kept this up for quite a while until one of the deacons got suspicious and went outside to see if he could find out what the preacher was doing when he stepped outside. The deacon found the whiskey, took the bottle up, drank some of it, and then put it in his coat pocket. Shortly after the deacon returned the preacher said his little say again and went outside. As usual, he looked under the steps, but his bottle of whiskey was not there. So this time when he went back in the church he got up and said:

> Don't sing another song,
> Don't say another prayer,
> 'Cause somebody here
> Done stole my fresh air.

GOD'S GIFTS TO THE FAITHFUL SISTERS *

De four best church members in de St. James Baptist Church, what was near de forks o' de road where de pavement

---

* Helen H. Sewell, "Folktales from a Georgia Family" (unpublished MA thesis, Indiana University, 1963) pp. 30-31, gives a somewhat different tale in which newcomers to heaven are given automobiles of different makes.

starts to head into Raleigh 'bout nine miles out, was Sister Mary Jones, Sister Janie Thompson, Sister Rosie Brown, an' Sister Liza Perkins. Dey wasn't nothin' dese four sisters wouldn't do for de church an' de preacher. Dey always set on de front row in de middle o' de church-house where dey could hear ever word de preacher say, an' den, too, he always called on one o' dese sisters to lead de prayer.

Durin' de time o' de Number One Worl' War, when de flu was on a rampage an' people was dyin' wid it ever hour in de day, all four o' dese sisters was in de bunch. So dey all goes up to Heaven an' St. Peter lets 'em in an' takes 'em up to God's thone. God done lef' word to bring 'em to him soon as dey gits dere, 'cause he say dey done led such a good Christian life 'till he wanna give 'em sumpin' nother for bein' so faithful. So when dey gets to God's thone an' courtesies, He call Sister Mary up an' say, "Sister Mary, you's been such a good Christian—not makin' over one or two mistakes durin' yo' whole lifetime—dat I'm gonna give you a Cadillac car to ride 'roun' in whilst you's up here." So Sister Mary thanks Him an' gets in de car an' drives on off. De nex' sister he called up was Sister Janie Thompson, so He say, "Sister Janie, you's been such a faithful servant down on earth 'till I wants to give you sumpin' to get 'roun' in whilst you's up here in Heaven." So He gives Sister Janie a Buick an' she thanks Him an' jumps in it an' drives on off. De nex' sister dat He called up was Sister Rosie Brown, so He say, "Sister Rosie, you ain't been quite as faithful as Sister Mary an' Sister Janie, but I's gonna reward you jus' de same, so here's a Ford for you." So Sister Rosie thanks Him an' gets in de car an' drives on off. Den God calls up Sister Liza Perkins an' say, "Sister Liza, you ain't been as faithful as de rest of 'em, but I's got a little car for you to ride 'roun' in, too." So God gives her a little Austin. But as soon as Sister Liza seed de little Austin she started laughin' loud as she can.

God don't know de why Sister Liza laughin' so hard, so he say, "Sister Liza, how come you laughin' like dat? Don't you like de car I done give you?"

"Yassuh, I likes it fine," say Sister Liza. "I wasn't laughin' at de car—I was laughin' 'cause I jus' seent my preacher go by on a scooter."

HOW "C. C. RIDER" CAME INTO EXISTENCE

I done heerd lots of people say dey like to have de knowledge to know how de song dat go by de name of "C. C. Rider" come to be.

Well, de way I heered it was like dis. Dey say dat right after we was freed dey used to have lots o' preachers goin' 'round from place to place dat traveled on horseback an' dey went 'round preachin' in de open 'fo' dey have arbors an' church-houses builded. Dey was solid against sin, an' dey specially don't like de songs de minstrel men sings an' de jokes dey crack. So dey tells de peoples to stop 'tendin' de minstrel shows what come through under de big tents, an' de people pays heed to 'em an' de minstrel shows have to go out o' business, 'cause dey ain't nuff peoples tendin' 'em to pay dey help.

So one of de minstrel mens what lose his job make up a song 'bout de circuit rider done put de minstrel shows out o' business. In dis song, "C. C. Rider, see what you done done," one of de C's was for Church, nother one was for Circuit. It mean, "Church Circuit Rider, see what you done done."

An dat's how de song come to be writ, an' dem what tells it say it was writ right here in North Carolina.

WHY DOOGER WOODS CHANGED HIS TEXT *

Dooger Woods was quite a character. He was pastor of
the Sugar Hill Baptist Church in Caldwell County, but had
been born and raised in the adjoining county, Wilkes, which
was called by people living in Caldwell County, because of
its bigness, "the State of Wilkes."

Dooger was one of the most talked-of characters in Caldwell County. He was a good friend of my father's and
grandfather's, and I could say of mine too, because I knew
him quite well and used to talk to him all the time when
I was a boy.

They say that Dooger was unable to read and write, but
he had a good memory and a powerful voice. My grandfather said that one Sunday morning when Dooger got
ready to deliver a sermon that he had prepared he looked
out into the congregation and saw a Negro man from
Wilkes County named Edward who knew him before he
started preaching and was a sinner. So, as grandfather tells
it, as soon as old Dooger saw Edward he said, "Now,
brothers and sisters, you knows sometime a preacher fix it
in his mind what he gonna preach about before he gets to
de church, an' after he gets dere he see somebody or sump'n
nother an' switch his mind clear around about what he gonna
preach about. Dat's de 'dickment I find myself in dis
mornin'. It done come to me right out o' de blue to change
my tex'; so I'm gonna change my tex' dis mornin' to de
second chapter o' de Book of Edward, which say, 'To all
dem dat sees me and knows me, say nothin' an' do nothin'
till I sees 'em later.' "

---

* Fauset found this same tale, using different names, in Nova
Scotia. See *Nova Scotia,* p. 94. Cf. Motif K1961.1.2.1. "Parody
sermon."

Puns and Comic Misunderstandings

THE PREACHER AND THE BOARD MEETING *

A country minister around Mocksville ended his sermon and then announced that he would like to have all the Board to remain for a few minutes. A stranger in the village who had worshipped at the church that morning made his way to the front pew and seated himself with the deacons and elders.

The minister approached him and said, "My dear sir, perhaps you misunderstood. I asked that only the Board remain."

"Well, that included me too," replied the stranger, "'cause I was never mo' bored in my life."

ONE WASN'T SAD †

A little boy up at Siler City had for a long time been asking his father to buy him a bicycle; but every time he'd ask his father'd reply, "I'll get you one as soon as I get straightened out."

The little boy asked his father this question every day for two years. His father's reply would always be the same— "I'll get you a bicycle as soon as I get straightened out." But one day the little boy's father died, and he still hadn't

---

* Cf. Motif J2495. "Religious words or exercises interpreted with absurd literalness."

† Cf. Motif J2470. "Metaphors literally interpreted."

54

bought him the bicycle he had been asking for. So at the funeral services, when the little boy's mother and all of his father's relatives and friends were crying, the little boy was laughing out loud, and clapping his hands with glee.

His mother, noticing his actions, turned to him angrily and said, "What's the matter with you—laughin' out loud, and clappin' yo' hands like that at yo' papa's funeral, when everybody else is sad?"

"I'm laughin' 'cause I'm happy," replied the little boy. "You see, papa said as soon as he got straightened out, he was gonna get me a bicycle, an' he's sho straightened out now."

UNCLE HENRY'S LOGIC *

"Boy," said Uncle Henry, a deeply religious man who lived out at Pleasant Grove, addressing his nephew, "how come you never reads de Bible? Don't you know you should read de Good Book and keep up with its teachin'?"

"I never does read de Bible," replied the nephew, " 'cause I figures it's jes' for de white folks and not for niggers. Dat's what I thinks."

"Boy, you're jes' ignorant," exclaimed Uncle Henry. "De Bible is for all good people, an' de color of dey skin don't make no difference. Where did you get de idea dat the Bible ain't for niggers?"

"Well," replied the boy, "fur as I can read, dey ain't no niggers in de Bible—nothing but white folks. Dat's why I says it's a white folks' Bible and not for niggers."

"You jes' proves what I been sayin', dat you is ign'ant,"

---

* Cf. Motif J1262.4. "Levity regarding Biblical passages."

said Uncle Henry, "cause if you read the scriptures you musta read 'bout one nigger name Demus—Niggerdemus."

THE UNMARRIED WOMAN AT THE PRAYER TREE *

Long time ago out in de rurals people used to go out in de woods when dey wanted sumpin' nother, an' pick 'em out a tree an' bow down on dey knees underneaf it, an' pray to God to send 'em what dey wanted. Dese trees go by de name of "prayer trees."

One time dey was a woman what done bypass de marryin' age, 'cause her mama an' papa done died when she was sixteen, an' since she was de oldest she have to take care of her li'l brothers an' sisters an' raise 'em till dey growed into de shape of men an' women an' could hustle for deyse'f. When de las' one of 'em done gone out in de worl' for deyse'f, she begin to get lonesome. But she forty-five now, an' her chances for gettin' married putty slim. She tell one of her friends dat she b'lieve she gonna get married, but dey ain't nobody in dem parts dat wants to get hitched to her. Her friend say for her to go down in de woods at night an' pick her out a prayer tree an' get down on her knees an' ask de Lord to send her a husband. So dat ver' nex' night de

---

* This tale should probably be considered a special form or subtype of Type 1476. Baughman classifies it as Motif J1811.1.1. "The old maid answers the owl's hoots, saying 'Anybody, Lord.'" A North Carolina Negro version is in E. C. Parsons, "Guildford County," p. 194. Other versions may be found in A. W. Eddins, "Anecdotes from the Brazos Bottoms," *Publications of the Texas Folklore Society*, XIII (1937), 97-98; H. Halpert, "Indiana Folktales," *Hoosier Folklore Bulletin*, I (1942), 28; and H. Halpert, "Folktales and Legends from the New Jersey Pines" (unpublished Ph.D. dissertation, Indiana University, 1947), pp. 476-477, 693.

woman goes down in de woods, picks her out a tree, an' gets down on her knees an' say, "Lord, please send me a man. Lord, please send me a man." Dere was a old hoot-owl settin' on one of de tree limbs she was under. He say, "Who? Who?" Den de woman say, "Praise de Lawd, praise de Lawd, my prayer done been answered." So de old hoot-owl say again, "Who? Who?" an' de woman say, "I don't care who it be, Lord, just since it's a man."

THE NORTH CAROLINA NEGRO AND
THE ALABAMA DEPUTY SHERIFF

One time a colored fellow who lived in Durham bought him a new Oldsmobile. Since he had a girlfriend who lived in Mobile, Alabama, he decided to drive the car down to Mobile so she could see it.

Everything went along all right until he ran into a curb near a little town in northern Alabama, and punctured one of his front tires. He got out of the car and was jacking up the wheel, when a deputy sheriff drove up in his car, jumped out of it, and ran over to where the colored fellow was changing his tire. He said, "Hey nigger, what you doin'?"

"Fixin' my automobile."

"What kind is it?"

"Oldsmobile."

"Where you goin', nigger?"

"Mobile."

"What's your name?"

"Henry Keel."

"What's your girl's name?"

"Lucille."

"What's that I'm gonna make you run across?"

"A cornfiel'."

About that time the sheriff heard a "click, click," and said, "What's that, nigger?"

"Forty-five blue steel," said the colored fellow, pointing the gun in the sheriff's face. "Now let me see you take to your heels, and start runnin' through that cornfiel'."

THE MOTHER'S LAST WORDS TO HER SON IN THE COUNTRY *

One time there was an old Negro lady who had a son that she tried to rear to be a very respectable young man.

When the son became twenty-one years old he left her and went to live in town. While he was in town he got in trouble and had to go to court. The court sentenced him to death in the electric chair.

The son was carried home to see his mother for the last time. When they got there, the guards asked her to say her last words to him.

She looked at her son and said, "Now, John, you know I have tried to raise you like good people. So you just go on down there and get 'lectrocuted, and then come on back home and act like you got some sense."

HOME ON THE HOG

One time dere was a boy right here in Rowan County what's brothers an' sisters was always pickin' on him, 'cause he was de littlest one in de fam'ly. Dey have a jealous

---

* Cf. Motif J2174. "Foolish demands before death."

streak, 'cause his mammy an' pappy was always buyin' de little fella sumpin' nother dat de big chilluns didn't get. So de big 'uns make life kinda hard for de little chap. But when dey all grows up dey leaves and makes dey way up de country somewhere, 'cause dey don't lack de way dey mammy an' pappy carryin' on over de littlest boy.

Den finally, de littlest boy grows up in de shape of a man, likewise, an' he 'cide dat he wanna go up de country, too, to see if'n he can hitch horses wid de peoples in New York, lack his big brothers an' sisters done did.

But his mammy and pappy gettin' old now, an' dey cautions wid him to stay on wid 'em on de li'l farm dey owns so's to be dey company keeper, but de little chap say, give him a try an' see how he can make out, an' den if'n he see he can't lick de big town he gonna trace his footsteps back to de farm.

De littlest boy gets long all right for a spell, but when it come to be Hoover Day, an' de 'Preshum hit de country, he lose his job. So he write his mammy an' pappy an' ask 'em to please sen' him some money to come home on, dat he up dere in New York City on de "Hog." So his mammy an' pappy reads de letter, an' sets right down an' answer him in dis wise:

"Dear Son, We hasn't got no money to send you to come home on, but since you's on de hog, just git on him an' ride him on home, 'cause we's had a bad crop dis year, an' we sho can use de meat."

HEADED FOR THE POORHOUSE

Durin' of Hoover Day, when times was harder dan a bed of rock coal, I was workin' two or three days ever week down to de Badin mills. Durin' dis time I rooms wid a old couple by de name of Mama Pitts an' Papa Pitts, what have a son dat work wid me dat go by de name of Bubber Pitts.

Mama an' Papa Pitts fare putty good, 'cause Papa Pitts was knowed real good down at de Badin mills; he work dere when he a young man, so de owner o' de mill take care o' Papa Pitts by takin' all de odd pennies what was lef' over from de pay o' de millworkers ever week, an' give 'em to Papa Pitts. Dis come to be almos' de equal to de salary we gets for three days' work at de mill. Den, too, dere boy Bubber he draw de same pay envelope we draws, so de Pitts family doin' awright for hisse'f.

But times 'gin to get tougher an' tougher; so me an' some more fellers, Bubber Pitts in de bunch, 'cides we gonna take a hobo trip up de country an' see if'n we can't get a regular job. We makes it as far up as Baltimore an' pops luck on de job situation. We all works hard an' saves our money, 'cep'n Bubber, who tuck his money ever Saddy night an' went down in de flats, an' spen' ever livin' cent he done made durin' de week. Finally, one day de plant where we was workin' close down unexpected like an' catch Bubber wid no money in his pocket.

So he hurries a letter to Mama Pitts an' Papa Pitts an' ask dem to sen' him some money to come home on. But de Badin mills done closed down, an' Papa Pitts an' Mama Pitts ain't gettin' no mo' left-over pennies. So dey doesn't have no money. Of a consequence dey hurries Bubber a letter back an' tells him dat dey don't have no money an' dat dey's gettin ready to go to de poorhouse tomorrow. So Bubber sets right down an' hurries dem a letter back an' say, "Don't y'all go to de poorhouse tomorrow. Y'all wait till I gets dere nex' week so I can go wid you."

THE INTELLIGENT SLAVE *

Durin' slavery time dere was a rich old massa in Brunswick County what owned mo'n three hundred slaves. Among dese slaves was one very smart slave named Tom. What I mean by smart is dat he was a smooth-operator—he knew what was happenin'. De way he come to be smart was by crawlin' under de massa's house ever night and listenin' to de massa tell his wife what kind o' work he was gonna have dey slaves do de next day. When de massa would come out o' de house ever mornin' an' get ready to tell de slaves what kind o' work he wanted dem to do dat day, Old Tom would say, "Wait just a minute, Massa. I knows zactly what you's gonna have us do today."

So de massa would stop talkin' an' let Old Tom tell de slaves what he had in mind for 'em to do dat day. Old Tom could always tell de slaves zactly what de massa wanted 'em to do, too; so de old massa was very much surprised, 'cause he didn't know how Old Tom was gettin' his information.

De reason Old Tom would go under de house ever night an' find out what de massa was gonna do de next day was

*For the introduction in which the slave overhears his master's conversation and pretends to foretell the future, see Dorson, *Michigan*, pp. 51-52 and 209, n. 20. The rest of the story is a widely known international tale, Type 1562A, "The Barn Is Burning." K. Jackson and E. Wilson, "The Barn Is Burning," *Folk-Lore*, XLVII (1936), 190-202, discuss European and especially British versions of the story. They cite two New York versions, p. 200. Dorson, *Michigan*, pp. 73-74, 215, n. 42, gives a Michigan Negro version and cites two other unpublished texts. He gives other important references including one to Hurston, pp. 109-110.

'cause he wanted to prove to his massa dat he was de smartest slave on de plantation. The smartest slave always got de easiest work on de plantation, and Old Tom was tired o' workin' hard. Sometimes de massas let dere smart slaves sleep in a bed in de Big House, too; so Old Tom had been dreamin' about one day, maybe, he would get to sleep in a real bed instead o' on a old quilt on his cabin floor. And it wasn't long before his dream come to be true, 'cause dat next comin' week after Old Tom done started prophesyin' de work for de slaves ever day, de old massa tell his wife dat he think he gonna bring Old Tom to live in de house wid dem, an' give him a room to sleep in. So dat next comin' mornin' he moved Old Tom in de house wid him an' his wife. Old Tom was so tickled he didn' know what to do wid hisse'f—just think, livin' in de same house wid his old massa.

One winter night when de massa an' his wife were seated around de fire de massa called Old Tom in to test his smartness. He pointed to de fire an' said, "Tom, what is dat?"

"Dat's a fire, massa," said Tom.

"No, it ain't either," replied his old massa. "Dat's a flame of evaporation." Just den a cat passed in front o' de fire, and de old massa say, "Tom, do you know what dat was dat just passed in front o' the fireplace?"

"Dat's a cat, sir," replied Tom.

Then his old massa said, "No it ain't neither. Dat's a high-ball-a-sooner."

Old Tom was gettin' tired o' answerin' questions by dis time, so he goes over to de window an' starts lookin' out. De old massa walk over to de window where Tom was an' say, "Tom, what is dat you's lookin' at out de window?"

"I's lookin' at a haystack," say Tom.

Den old massa say, "Dat ain't no haystack. Dat's a high-tower."

Den Old Tom set down in a chair an' started gettin' ready to go to his room up in de attic and go to bed for de night. He didn' wanna get de carpet all spotted up wid dirt in de livin' room, so he started to unbucklin' his shoes and takin' 'em off. When de old massa looked an' seen Tom takin' off his shoes, he say, "What's dem, Tom?" An' Tom say, "Dem's my shoes."

"No, dey ain't neither," say his old massa. "Dem dere's yo' tramp-tramps." Den de old massa pointed through the archway to where a bed could be seed in his bedroom, and said, "What's dat dere I's pointin' to in dere, Tom?" "Dat's a bed," say Old Tom.

"No, it ain't neither," said his old massa; "Dat's a flowery bed of ease, an' I's goin' right now, and get in it, 'cause we's all got a hard day's work comin' up tomorrow." So de old massa an' de old missus goes on in dey bedroom an' goes to bed. Den Old Tom goes on up to de li'l attic room where dey lets him sleep an' gets in bed.

But just as Tom started to get in his bed de cat runned through de fire in de fireplace and caught on fire, and run out to de haystack and set it on fire. Old Tom run to de window an' looked out and seed de cat on fire, an' de haystack on fire, so he started yellin' as loud as he could, "Massa, Massa, you better get up out of yo' flowery bed of ease, an' put on yo' tramp-tramps 'cause yo' high-ball-a-sooner done run through yo' flame of evaporation an' set yo' high-tower on fire." His old massa didn't move a peg—he just hunched his wife an' said, "Lissen at dat high-class slave up there usin' all of dat Latin."

Den once mo' Old Tom yell out, "Massa, Massa, I say dat you better get up out of yo' flowery bed of ease, an' put on yo' tramp-tramps, 'cause yo' high-ball-a-sooner done run through yo' flame of evaporation an' set yo' high-tower on fire." But Tom's old massa just hunched his wife again, an' say, "Dat sho is a smart slave, dat Tom, ain't he? Just listen at him talkin' all dat Latin up dere again."

Old Tom went on yellin' like dis about five more times, but when he seed dat his old massa wasn't gettin' out of bed he yelled, "Massa, you better git up out of dat bed, an' put yo' damn shoes on, an' go out dere an' put dat haystack fire out dat yo' cat done started, or else yo' whole damn farm's gonna burn up."

THE TOBACCO STACKER'S MISTAKE

One year, during tobacco-stacking time, a tobacco grower near Winston-Salem brought some Negroes up from Georgia to stack his tobacco for him. The reason he did this was that he could hire the Georgia Negroes cheaper.

The Georgia Negroes had heard about how bad Winston-Salem Negroes were, so every Saturday when they got their week's pay they would slip off, two or three at a time, and go into town and buy guns, knives, and wine. The reason they could not stay in town long at a time was that they worked all day Saturday—they just got paid off at ten o'clock in the morning and had two hours off for the day—from ten to twelve.

There was one in the bunch who never went into town but who'd always send by some of the others for a quart of "Eleven Star" wine every Saturday. He kept up this practice for about four weeks, but finally, on the fifth Saturday after they had started to work on the tobacco farm, he decided that he'd go into town himself and get his "Eleven Star" wine. When he got there he went into the first store he saw, which was a hardware store, and told the owner that he wanted

a bottle of "Eleven Star" wine. The owner said, "We don't
have nothin' but hardware here."

So the Negro said, "Well, gimme a bottle of that."

THE SPELLING BEE AND
THE COUNTY SUPERINTENDENT

My gran'ma say when she was a little bitty girl jes' startin'
to school out to Tobaccoville, dat dey jes' hab a one-room
school wid one teacher, and dat mos' o' de little school
scholars was boys. Some o' de little boys' names was Tom
Miller, Jimmy Brown, Bob Thomas, Chuck Connor, Ray-
mond Moore, and Bill Johnson, but dey was one little fellow
dat was named Damn-it Jones.

Gran'ma say dat little Damn-it was a top scholar in rif-
metic—dat he could work wid figgers real good, but dat he
was at de bottom o' de class when it come to spellin' day.
Gran'ma say dey'd have a "spellin' bee" ever Friday jes' 'fo'
school turned out, and dat little Damn-it was always at de
bottom o' de row.

One Friday, howbeever, gran'ma say, de County Sup'inten't comed by de school an' tuck him a seat whilst dey
was havin' de spellin' match. Gran'ma say dat her an' de
other li'l girls an' all de boys spelled all de words de teacher
give out till finally de teacher ask 'em to spell de word
Nebuchadnezzar an' dey all missed out, cep'n she ain't got
to Damn-it Jones yet, so li'l Damn-it riz up his han' real
high in de air an say, "Teacher, let me spell it."

"Damn-it Jones, you can't spell it," say de teacher, an'
when she say dis de sup'inten't stan' up real quick and say,
"Hell, teacher, let him try!"

Tales of the Wise and Foolish

THE DEPUTY SHERIFF AND THE NEGRO BOOTLEGGER

Negro bootleggers from Wilkes County were very hard to catch. Most of 'em always went down to Winston-Salem or Greensboro or Raleigh to sell their mash. One of the smartest of these bootleggers did most of his sellin' in Winston-Salem, but as is always the case, some member of his own race told a deputy sheriff about this Negro and pointed him out one day when the bootlegger had finished disposing of his liquor.

The deputy sheriff found out what part of town the Wilkesboro Negro operated in, however, and the days that he came into town to sell his liquor. So the very next day that the Negro was scheduled to come to Wilkesboro to sell liquor the sheriff disguised himself, walked up to him, and asked him if he knew where he could get some good home-made whiskey.

"How much do you want?" asked the Negro.

"About five dollars' worth," replied the sheriff.

"Well gimme the five dollars," said the Negro, "and I'll go and see what I can do."

"Here," said the Negro before leaving, handing the deputy sheriff a shoe box, "hold these shoes for me till I git back."

The sheriff took the shoebox and waited for three hours, but the Negro never returned. So he decided to look in the box and see what was in it. When he opened it up, there was a fifth of bootleg liquor.

SOMEBODY HAD TO PUT A STOP TO IT

One time during of de Number Two Worl' War two fellows settin' down in a barbershop was talkin' 'bout what de Japs was doin' in de War. De first one say, "De Japs bombed San Francisco las' mont'."

"Say dey did?" say de second one.

"Yeah, an' dey bombed New York City las' week," say de first one.

"Say dey did?" say de second one.

"Yeah, an' dey bombed New Orleans yesterday," say de first one.

"Well, dey ain't gonna bomb Kannapolis," say de second one.

"How come dey ain't?" say de first one.

" 'Cause Mr. Cannon ain't gonna let 'em," say de second one.

LOVE I SEE, LOVE I STAND, LOVE I HOLDS IN MY RIGHT HAND *

Long time ago, 'fo' de blue coats what dey call Yankees come roamin' 'roun', things was rockin' 'long putty good here

---

* This riddle tale, one of the best known of the so-called "neck-saving riddles," is classified under Type 927. In a useful comparative article, "The Prisoner Who Saved His Neck with a Riddle," *Folk-Lore*, LIII (1942), F. J. Norton gives examples of the "Love" riddle from England, Bermuda, Germany, Denmark, and other European countries (pp. 35-41). The story, or just the riddle alone, has been collected frequently in the United States from both Negro and white informants. The following list is only a selection of refer-

betwixt de slaves an' dey old massas. Lots of de massas lack to carry on foolishness wid dey slaves, speshly when it rain, an' it get too wet to work in de 'bacco fields.

One time up 'roun' New Bern dey was a good old massa what have a slave name Joe, what he like to joke wid all de time. Him an' Joe was always swappin' jokes, an' riddles, so one day he say, "Massa, you gimme a riddle to figger out today, so spose'n I brings you one in de mornin', an' if'n you can't guess what de answer be you give me my freedom."

"Awright Joe," say de old massa, "if'n you can bring me a riddle what I can't figger out I'll sho give you yo' freedom."

So dat nex' comin' mornin' 'fo' daybreak Old Joe knocks on de old massa's door, an' de massa, what already done got out of bed an' put on his clothes, say, "Come on in Joe. Has you got dat riddle you was tellin' me you gonna bring wid you dis mornin'?"

"I sho has," say Joe, who done killed his old dog what named Love de night befo', an' what done take an' cut him up an' take a piece o' his skin an' wrap 'roun' his right hand. So he say, "Yassuh, I's got de riddle all set to go."

"Well awright den," say de old massa, "let's have it."

"Well den, here she go," say Joe:

"Love I see; Love I stan';
Love I holds in my right han'."

"Now, what dat be, massa?" say Joe.

ences to American versions. Negro: North Carolina, Parsons, "Guildford County" p. 203 (two versions); South Carolina, *Journal of American Folklore*, XXXIV (1921), 26-27; Parsons, *Sea Islands*, pp. 157-158; Louisiana, *Journal of American Folklore*, XXXVIII (1925), 281; Nova Scotia, Fauset, p. 142. White: North Carolina, *Journal of American Folklore*, XLVII (1934), 322-323 (two versions); Southern Mountains, *Journal of American Folklore*, XLVII (1934), 77; Ozarks, *Journal of American Folklore*, XLVII (1934), 82.

Joe's old massa try hard as he can to guess de riddle, but he don't never come up wid de rat answer. So after-while he say, "Joe, I gives up, so I's gonna give you yo' freedom, but 'fo' I gives it to you I wants you to do me one favor: tell me what de answer to de riddle be."

"Sho, Massa, sho," say Joe. "You see dis here brown piece of skin I's got in my right han'? Dat's a piece of my old dog's skin name of Love.

"All de time I was talkin' to you I was stannin' dere wid it, an' I was holdin' it in my han' lookin' at it. So dat's why I says:

"Love I see; Love I stan';

Love I holds in my right han'."

UNCLE CHARLEY'S REPORT ON HORSE EATING *

One time here in Raleigh, 'reckly after de Yankees done come 'roun' an' take everthing dey could get dey hands on, an' dey have what dey call drummers comin' 'roun' sellin' a whole lots of diffunt things, dey builded a lots of what dey called livery stables, where dey hire out horses an' buggies to dese drummers what rent 'em to drive to all de little bitty towns an' country stores what scattered roundabouts in de county.

One of dese livery stables hire a old colored man by de name of Uncle Charley to 'tend to de horses, hitch 'em up to de buggies, an' feed 'em. De man what run de livery stable didn't have nothin' but black horses an' white horses; so he name his livery stable "De Black an' White Livery Stable." It come to be real pop'lar wid de drummers, an' evertime

---

* Cf. Motif J2030. "Absurd inability to count."

one'd hit Raleigh dey'd come right to de Black and White an' rent a horse an' buggy.

All de drummers knowed Uncle Charley, 'cause he was always so polite an' kept de horses' harness shine up pretty an' clean. De boss-man lack it 'cause de drummers lack him so good. So he give Uncle Charley leeway to make reports to him 'bout diffunt things. Ever mornin' Uncle Charley'd have sumpin' nother to report to de boss-man, an' de reports was all true. Things go along pretty good for a long time, an' Uncle Charley don't never make no false reports.

But dis here too good to be true. Uncle Charley makin' too good a headway for it to las' too long. So one mornin' when de boss-man comed into de stable Uncle Charley say, "Boss, I wants to report dat de black horses is eatin' more feed dan de white horses is."

"Say dey is?" 'low de boss-man. "Well, I better look into dis here thing." So he looks aroun' de stable at de horses and den come back to where Uncle Charley is settin' on a bale of hay an' say, "Charley, I done found out why de black horses eats more dan de white horses. Dey's more black horses in de stable dan dey is white 'uns; dey's twenty-four black 'uns, and ain't but twelve white 'uns."

JESSE JAMES AND THE BURIED MONEY *

It is said that Jesse James, the famous robber, robbed a bank one time in North Carolina, right after slavery time,

---

* In a Negro tale from Philadelphia, a Negro buries money in a graveyard and puts a gravestone above it reading "Dead and Buried." A Jew has watched him. He digs it up and changes the message to "Rose and Gone to Glory." A. H. Fauset, "Tales and Riddles Collected in Philadelphia," *Journal of American Folklore*, XLI (1928), 551. Pertinent motifs include J2091.1. "Fool hides treasure and leaves sign, 'Here it is.' Thief leaves sign, 'Here it is not.' " K439.10. "Hidden person sees robbers concealing treasure and takes it." N511.1.1. "Treasure buried in graves."

and wanted to hide the money, but he did not know where to hide it. His brother Frank told him to hide it in the colored graveyard, because all the ex-slaves were afraid of dead folks, and the money would be safe there.

What Jesse and Frank did not know was that a Negro runaway from justice was hiding out in the graveyard, and that when he saw Jesse and Frank coming he went and climbed up in a tree and hid.

Jesse buried the money and put a sign over it which read, "Dead and Buried." After Jesse and Frank left, the Negro dug up the money, took it, and made his escape.

When Jesse returned for the money several months later the sign read, "Risen and Gone."

THE COTTON FARMER *

(In Harrison Neal's own words and of his own telling to the author)

Fred McCullough, what jes' passed a little while back, told me dis here, but dis ain't no story; it's de truth. Fred used to love to tell it all de time, and he'd jes' crack his sides a-laughin' 'bout how he got out of South. Carolina.

You know settin' 'round listenin' to old people talk you can learn lots of things, if you's a chap—dat is if you don' look up in a grown person's face. (A chap ain't supposed to look up in a grown person's face less'n dey sign you to come on; dey'd whip you to death about dat when I was comin' up.)

---

*This same tale was given by C. S. Johnson, *et al.*, *The Collapse of Cotton Tenancy*, p. 9, and reprinted by Botkin, p. 80. For other tales in which a white landowner makes his tenants' accounts come out even, see Brewer, *The Word on the Brazos*, pp. 92-93, and Dorson, *Pine Bluff*, pp. 119-120.

Anyway, gettin' back to Fred McCullough, and how he got out of South Carolina, when a push come to a shove. Fred say him an' two more fellows was croppin' on a cotton farm down in South Carolina what was owned by Mr. Bub-Ub-Um, an' dat Mr. Bub-Ub-Um have a store where dey trade, an' a office where he figger up how much cotton dey done raise ever year. Dey always comed out in de hole an' have to stay on de farm till dey raise enough bales of cotton to break dead even.

Fred say dat de fus' three years him an' "Roun' House" an' "Dennis" raise cotton, Mr. Bub-Ub-Um would take out his pencil an' a piece of paper in de little narrow office he had, an' when dey tell him how many bales dey done made dat year he say, rubbin' his chin wid his hand, "Well, lemme see. You know you done putty good dis year. You jes' lacked five bales of breakin' dead even. Maybe nex' year you'll break dead even."

When de fo'th year roll roun' it was a putty good crop year an' dey made more cotton dan ever before. So Fred say when he got dere Mr. Bub-Ub-Um say, "Well, Roun' House, how many bales did you make dis year?"

"I made seven bale," say Roun' House.

"Well, now, considerin' dat you ain't had nobody to help you but yo' wife dat was real good," say Mr. Bub-Ub-Um, "but you jes' lack three bales of bein' straight. Maybe next year you'll get straight."

Dennis was de next 'un go to settle up wid Mr. Bub-Ub-Um. So when he go to settle up Mr. Bub-Ub-Um say, "Dennis how many bales did you raise dis year?"

Dennis say, "I done raise ten bales."

"Well, well," say Mr. Bub-Ub-Um, strokin' his chin wid his hand like he always do, "you did fine, Dennis. You had a lot o' help dis year—six big children to hoe and chop and pick, so you broke dead even."

"Well dat's good," say Dennis. "Since I done broke even I think I'll go to work some place else. Maybe I kin hit it off a little better." So Dennis pack up his clothes an' lef'.

De las 'un to go settle up wid Mr. Bub-Ub-Um was Fred. Fred done raise twelve bales of cotton, but he ain't gonna tell Mr. Bub-Ub-Um he raise but ten bales, an' hold back two. So when he go back to settle up, Mr. Bub-Ub-Um ask him how many bales of cotton he done raise dis year. Fred tell he done raise ten bales like Dennis. So Mr. Bub-Ub-Um say, "Well, well, you done putty good dis year too, Fred. You broke dead even."

"Well, dat's good," say Fred, "but dere's two mo' bales I didn't tell you 'bout."

"The hell you did," yelled Mr. Bub-Ub-Um, grabbin' de sheet o' paper he figurin' on, tearin' it up, an' pointin' his finger in Fred's face. "Don't you never do nothin' like dat again, nigger. Have me refigurin' yo' crop all over so you can come out dead even."

Fred jes' walk on off and don't say nothin', but dat same night when it done come to be pitch dark Fred took two of Mr. Bub-Ub-Um's best mules an' a fine Jersey cow, filled a sack full of Mr. Bub-Ub-Um's bes' chickens, an' started out walkin' towards Spencer. He come straight on here to Spencer an' lived here de rest of his nachul bawn life.

THE CHEROKEE INDIAN AND THE ASHEVILLE BANKER

When dey first signed a bank to come on into Asheville, a Cherokee Injun from de reservation heerd 'bout it an' comed into Asheville an' walked in de bank. He took a good look around an' den connected wid de bank clerk an' say, "Me want some money."

So de bank clerk say, "Has you got any money in de bank?" An' de Injun say, "No, me no got money in Bank."

So de bank clerk hurry de Injun a answer right back an' say, "Well den, does you wanna borry some money?"

So de Injun say, "Yep, me wanna borry money." So de bank clerk point out de bank president what am settin' behin' a railin' at 'tother end of de bank, an' say, "If'n you wanna borry some money, go'ver dere to dat man hin' dat railin' an' tell him you wants to."

So de Injun walks over to de railin' where de bank president readin' a paper an' say, "Me want money."

An' de bank president connect wid de Injun just like de clerk do an' say, "Has you got any money in de bank?"

"No," say de Injun, "me no got money in bank."

"Well, does you wanna borry some money?" say de bank president.

"Yep," say de Injun, "me wanna borry money."

"How much money does you wanna borry?" say de bank president.

"Ten thousand dollar," say de Injun.

"Ten thousand dollar?" say de bank president. "Does you have any collateral?"

"No understan' collateral," say de Injun.

"Well den," say de president, "does you own anything?"

"Yep," say de Injun, "me own four hundred horse and ten thousand acre of land."

So de bank president say all right, he'll let him have de money, and counts out ten thousand dollars an' han's 'em to de Injun.

Dat nex' comin' Saddy mornin' after de Injun done borry de money de bank president look up, an' who do he see comin' in de door but dat Injun what done borry de money de week 'fo' dis un.

De Injun walk straight over to de president's desk, digs down in his pocket, takes out some bills, an' counts out ten thousand dollars an' han's 'em to de president. De president can't hardly b'lieve what he see, 'cause de Injun stannin' dere holdin' 'nother ten thousand dollars in his han'. So de president eye de Injun a minute, after he get over his surprise. Den he say, "Look-a-here, Injun, dat's a mighty heap o' money for you to be carryin' 'roun' wid you. How about leavin' it here in de bank wid me?"

De Injun try his best to think of de word "collateral," but he can't recollect it. So he look de president dead straight in de eye an' say, "How many horse you got?"

THE INDIAN AND THE POLICEMAN

One time an Indian came to town off of the reservation and saw a policeman on a motorcycle. He had not been to town for a long time, so he did not know what a motorcycle was.

The policeman got off of the motorcycle and went into a nearby store, but before going into the store he saw the Indian looking at the motorcycle curiously. So he said over his radio attached to the motorcycle, "Don't bother my scooter while I am in the store, Indian!"

This made the Indian curious, so as soon as the policeman was out of sight he jumped on the motorcycle and started riding it, but he couldn't stop it, so he finally ran into a car, hurting himself and breaking the motorcycle.

When the policemen found him he said, "What happened, Indian? I told you to leave my scooter alone." So the Indian replied:

"Me no know,

Me can't tell;
Me push button,
And it run like hell."

HARRISON NEAL AND THE GAME WARDEN

As a spinner of tales Harrison Neal had no peer. This is the way he told the story about his encounter with a game warden during the depression era.

Way back in durin' of de time when Mr. Hoover done clap de panic on, I been cut offen my job fer a week in de Badin pot rooms. Man! De country 'roun' about here an' dere been kivvered up wid hard times. A white man tells me dat Mr. Hoover an' de chigger done shake dey han's on it dat dey gonna make it hard on everbody. If'n Mr. Chigger do he bes' to keep de po' folks outen from amongst de blackberry patches, den Mr. Hoover say he gonna do his bes' to keep de niggers an' de po' white trash outen work. Po' old Neal (me) ain't had de first dime. Once in awhile though, he gits job of work 'nuff to buy a little terbaccy. Man! If'n railroad engineers was a dime a dozen he ain't had 'nuff money to blow de whistle on one of 'em. I's sho makin' headway hind part foremost; good thing I ain't got nobody but myself to scratch for. Mammy an' de rest of de fam'ly done move offen de home place, an' I been livin' in a shack in Badin, but just de same I have to eat sum'n nother lack anybody else. An' gentlemens, if'n I hadn't of been on good terms wid de little fishes an' rabbits an' squirrels, old Neal would'a' had to git down on his all fours an' eat grass mo samer'n den any cow dat grazin' in de pasture. De chiggers done give up on me, cause po' old Neal ain't hardly got blood 'nuff for heself. Well, sir, one mornin' I wakes up 'long 'bout four o'clock an' my backbone feels lack it been workin' button holes in my stomach. So I lays dere takin' stock of myself, and putty soon I comes to de 'clusion dat if'n I wants breakfast dat mornin' I better go catch it out in de ribber. Man! I done et so many of dem little fishes an' little birds an' little rabbits till old Neal don't know whether he spose to swim or fly or walk. So after while I gits up offen de pallet I was sleepin' on, and goes out to last year's hog-pen what 'long to de white folks an' starts scramblin' 'roun' in de ground till I digs up a can full of worms. I always keeps some hooks in my hat brim, an' a ball of twine, an' a few taps for sinkers in my pants pocket, 'cause in dem days old Neal likely to go fishin' any time of de day or night.

So after I done dig my worms an' put 'em in de can, I sets out for a deep hole on the 'Gomery side of de ribber where de catfishes lays on de bottom, 'cause de weather been hotter'n any ginger mill a grindin' in hell. I gits down to de bank of de ribber where I keeps my batoe tied to a willow tree. I gits in de batoe and puts out across to de 'Gomery side, just below where de Whorrie an' de 'Adkin Ribbers joins up, an' I lands on de flat rock an' ties de batoe to a little birch tree what doin' it's bes' to split de big rock. I looks 'roun fo' de bes' place to fish, an' 'cides if'n I clams up de big rock rat over de deep hole I kin spy all 'roun' an' fish at de same time, 'cause dey was game wardens wanderin' all 'roun' dem parts to see if'n you had a license to ketch little fishes. I didn't see nary body an' didn't hear nary body; so I th'ows my pole in de water an' sits where I kin see any-body dat come up and down de footpaths 'long de ribber edge. Den I sets down an' rares back 'gin a big willow tree, an' den 'members dat I ain't et nothin' since de day before. But dere wasn't no food dere on de ribber; de mostes' an' de handies' thing to eat or drink was dat clear ribber water, so

I clams down from where I was settin' an' goes an' drinks 'bout a gallon of water. When I done drunk de water I starts to ramblin' 'roun' in my pockets an' comes out wid a chunk of sassyfras root to chaw on. Den I clams back up to my fishing place an' gits on wid what I come dere after. De little fishes know dat old Neal ain't had no breakfast, so dey goes outen dey way to get on my hook. 'Fo' long I has me a nice long string of little cats.

De little birds was singin' an' chirpin' in de thickets along de ribber banks—dey kin 'ford to sing 'cause dey little bellies is full an' dey ain't heerd nary a word 'bout de hand-shakin' agreement Mr. Hoover an' de chiggers done had. Long 'bout dis same time a old squirrel start to talkin' to heself way up on de bluff in de white oaks, an' a old jaybird put in his two cents' worth 'long wid de little birds what was singin' an' chirpin'. Den I looks up an' sees a old fishhawk hustlin' up his breakfast just like old Neal, an' I says to myself, "I ain't by myself after all, 'cause de old fish hawk out hustlin' mo' samer dan I is." Man! It sho been a putty mornin', old Neal at peace wid de worl'. Den I 'gin to git sleepy, but old Neal he sly like de fox—he keep his eyes rovin' 'roun' de country- side 'roun' abouts, an' he keep his ears pricked up like a old mammy rabbit wid a nest of young'uns. Man! Dat sho pay off after while, 'cause tain't long before I hears somebody's feetsteps goin' crash, crash, 'long on de grabbel 'long de foot- path what run up an' down de ribber. I knowed it been a game warden man, so I's scared stiff. I be's in 'Gomery County, an' ain't got no license to fish dere, an' no money to buy one, likewise. I knows de game warden ain't spy me yit, 'cause he ain't holler "Halt" lack de polices do when dey 'rests you. So I say to myself, "Neal, you got to do sumpin' fast." So I grabs up a stick, clamps it twixt my teeth dish here way;

I walls my eyeballs way back in my head dish here way, an' den falls down on de groun' slobberin' at de mouf an kickin' an' jerkin an' makin' de mos' awful sounds mo' samer'n a man havin' a lipilectic fit lack what I done seed. I hears dem footsteps comin' closer an' closer, an' putty soon dey gits 'bout ten or twelve feet from where I was layin' down an' dey stops. Den I squinted my eye an' seed a man 'bout dish here high. He was a game warden, sho 'nuff, an' he just stand dere an' stare at me from a safe distance back; so I knows dat he ain't gonna bother long wid no po' nigger wid no lipilectic fit. So he just look at me an' say, "Lord, help me!" an' wid dis he turn on his heels an' de las' I hear him his feets was goin' crash, crash on de grabbel in de footpaths what runs long up an' down de ribber. So old Neal he git up offen de groun', takes de stick outen his mouf, grabs de line, hook, tap, an' all offen de pole, grabs de fish, jumps in his batoe, an' paddles back to de Badin side. When I gits to de other side an' ties up my batoe an' clams up de steep bank, I sees Mr. John Webb in the garden. I howdys to him, an he 'sponds, likewise, den I havens up my fish wid 'im an' he gives me a hat full of 'matoes an' cucumbers, some roasinyears, an' a cabbage or two. Man! Dem be make fine breakfast sho nuff.

De nex' week I gits a day's work in de Badin pot room an' I hears a white man say dat he brother-in-law what live in 'Gomery County say dat he sho do be tired of bein' game warden, 'cause don't nobody break de law, but most everwhere dat you turns you just likely to run across some po' nigger havin' a lipilectic fit.

JIM JOHNSON AND HIS NEW SUIT OF CLOTHES

One Saddy long 'bout dusk dark, Jim Johnson what lived out to Five Row 'cided dat he wanna buy him a new suit o' clothes to go to de ball game what gonna be played at Mocksville dat next comin' Sunday.

All de big sto's on Main Street was closed—wasn't but one sto' open an' dat was a sto' runned by a Jew man, name Mr. Rubenstein. So Jim walks into de sto' and looks round, an' a putty blue serge suit finally catch his eye. He try on de suit an' it fit him jes' right. He pay fo' it, and Mr. Rubenstein wrap it up, and Jim carry it on home and hangs it on a nail on de wall. Sunday evenin' he take de suit down an' put it on, an' jumps in his ol' "T" model Ford, what ain't got no top on it, and drives up to Mocksville to see de Carolina Quick Steppers play de Mocksville Black Harnets.

De game ain't got started good, 'fo' it come up a big cloudburst, and Jim's suit o' clothes got soak an' wet from de rain. When he gits home he takes de suit off an' puts it on a ol' rockin' chair by de wood stove to dry. After de suit done dried off, Jim puts it on, an' de breeches comes way up twix his knees an' his ankles—when he put on de coat he couldn't button de buttons on it. So when Monday morning comes Jim puts on de suit an' goes down to Mr. Rubenstein's sto' to show him how de suit done drawed up.

When he git dere he goes in an' walks up to Mr. Rubenstein an' say, "Mr. Rubenstein, does you remember me, Jim?"

"Sho, I remembers you," say Mr. Rubenstein, pattin' Jim on de back, an' de suit of clothes all at de same time, "but my! how you has growed!"

Tales about Marriage

THE SHOWDOWN *

One time dere was a man what had a wife dat was low-sick. She done 'tracted consumption, an' de doctor say her days on earth was numbered. So her husban' was goin' 'roun' droopin', an' ever night he'd get down on his knees an' pray in dis here wise: "Lord, please don't take my wife; please take me in her place." He pray lack dis here ever night, an' one day when de preacher comed to have prayer wid his wife he met de preacher on his way outen de house an' say, "Revun, I don't want my wife to die; I wants to die in her place." So de preacher say, "Well, I tells you what.

I has a rooster dat b'longs to me what can point out de one what gonna die first in a house. So I tells you what I'll do; I gonna bring de rooster wid me tomorrow when I comes to pray wid yo' wife an' leave him at de front door. When he come in he gonna go in one of de rooms. So you be in 'nother room diffunt from yo' wife's when I gets here."

Dis here scare de man up putty much; so he don't sleep very well dat night. He get up bright an' early de nex' mornin', too, an' go an' get into d'other bedroom t'other side of de room where his wife at. Putty soon he hear de footsteps of de preacher. Den he listen, an' hear de rooster's footsteps pass on by his wife's bedroom door an' start toward his'n. So he jumps out of de bed real quick, reaches de door 'fo' de rooster can get dere, an' goes out in de hall. He meets de rooster comin' towards his room. So he rush up to where de rooster was real quick an' point to his wife's bedroom door an' whisper in de rooster's ear, "She's in dere, she's in dere."

TELL MY WIFE *

One Saddy me and some more fellows decided dat we'd go fishin' on de Yadkin; so we rented a boat an' started downstream. It had been rainin' a lots dat week, an' de water was pretty swift, but we decided we'd go on an' fish anyways.

We'd been rowin' 'roun' in de water 'bout a hour, I guess, when all of a sudden de boat struck a rock, or sumpin' nother, an' turned over. Dey was four of us in de bunch, an' all of us struck out to swimmin' towards de river bank, cep'n one, what was throwed head foremos' in de water when de boat keeled over. De lick he got when he hit de

---

* A similar tale is given by Hurston, p. 129.

water was so hard 'till it stunded him, an' he started sinkin' down to de bottom of de river. Ever time he'd come up he'd go down again. Ever time he'd come up he'd holler, "Tell my wife, tell my wife!"

We was all in a study as to how come he just hollerin', "Tell my wife, tell my wife," all de time, an' he don't never swim on outen de water like we done did, but we don't have de understandin' to know dat dere's a suck-hole in de river keep on pullin' him down ever time he come up. Finally, though, as de Lawd would have it, a big log come floatin' by jus' as he riz up outen de water, an' he grabbed it an' ketched hold of it, an' brung hisse'f to de river bank where we was settin' dere dryin' off.

When he got where we was we say, "What's dat you want us to tell yo' wife?" An' he say, "Dat's all right, I'll tell her myself now."

THE MOUNTAIN MAN AND HIS THREATENING WIFE *

One time there was an old mountain man and his wife who lived right over yonder near the top of the ridge in Possum Hollow, who had a little boy.

They were always fussin' an' fightin'. So one day in the winter time when snow was on the ground and the hills was all covered with ice, the mountain man's wife picked up a ax and tried to knock him in the head with it. So the man grabbed up his little nine-year-old boy, put on his mackinaw, wrapped a blanket around the little boy, and left the house and went and telephoned the sheriff in Wilkesboro to come and get his wife, because she had threatened to kill him.

---

* Cf. Motifs K1860. "Deception by feigned death (sleep)." T298. "Reconciliation of separated couple."

While the man was gone the woman went back home and thought she'd play a trick on her husband. So she took a bottle of blackberry juice, lay down on the floor of the cabin, and poured the juice all over her face, her hands, and her clothes, and pretended to be dead.

When the man got back with the boy he looked at her and was so scared he didn't know what to do. He was afraid to touch her, but pretty soon she got up off the floor and laughed about pretending to be dead, and promised her husband that she wouldn't threaten him no more.

When the sheriff got there he found the husband and wife sitting down at the table eating and laughing and talking.

When he saw what was happening—after walking ten miles through the ice and snow to reach the cabin—he was so angry that he arrested both of them, brought 'em down to Wilkesboro, and put 'em in jail.

SHE WASN'T THE FUSSY KIND

One time a colored woman named Carrie was workin' for my mother. Mother worked her about three days a week, over and above the laundry work she did for mother.

One day when Carrie got to work she looked at mama and said, "Missy, I's got to be off tomorrow; I can't come to work."

Mama was surprised, because Carrie had never asked to be off from work before. So she said, "Carrie, what you got to be off for?" And Carrie replied, "It ain't me, Missy. I's got to take my li'l boy to de doctor."

"Yo' little boy to de doctor," replied mother. "I thought you told me you was an old maid."

"Yassum, dat's what I is," said Carrie. "But I ain't the fussy kind."

Tales about Mountain Whites

THE MOUNTAIN MAN AND THE MIRROR *

One time a mountain man found a small mirror—the first one he'd ever seen. He looked in it and said with surprise, "By cracky, it's a pitcher of my old pappy."

Sentimentally, he hid the mirror under the bed. His wife saw him hiding it. When he went to work the next morning she went under the bed, took the mirror out, looked into it, and snorted, "So that's the old bag he's been chasin'."

BIG MOUNTAIN MAN AND LITTLE MOUNTAIN MAN

In a mountain town of North Carolina there lived a mountain man about eight feet, nine inches tall. One day a little fellow about five feet four walked up to him and said, "Man, if I was as big as you I would go up in the mountain and grab a big bear and whip him to death."

The big man looked down on him and said, "There's some little bears up there, too."

---

* This tale, which Baughman lists as Motif J1795. "Image in mirror mistaken for picture," has been collected in both England and the United States. See E. M. Wilson, "Some Humorous English Folk-Tales, Part Two," *Folk-Lore*, XLIX (1938), 277-278, and N. H. Thorp and N. M. Clark, *Pardner of the Wind* (Caldwell, Idaho, 1945), p. 209.

THE MOUNTAIN MAN AND THE MOTORCYCLE *

Right over there to the left on the side of the road lookin' over yo' right shoulder, in that li'l cabin up on the mountainside, was where my grandma's half-brother used to live. He was real handy with a shotgun and took a shot at everything he saw.

One evenin' just before sunset when it just was beginnin' to get dark, grandma's brother an' his wife was settin' out on a bench in front of the cabin when they looked up an' saw a man ridin' down the road on a motorcycle. They had never laid eyes on a motorcycle before; so they thought that it was some kind of animal from the noise it made and the way it looked. As soon as grandma's brother saw it, he grabbed up his shotgun that he had layin' on the ground next to the cabin steps and fired at the motorcycle. The buckshot hit the motorcycle and made it turn 'round and 'round on the ground, causing the man to fall off it.

When the motorcycle fell to the ground, grandma's brother's wife said, "Did you kill it?"

"No, I didn't kill it," he replied, "but I sho made it turn that man loose."

THE REVENUE AGENTS AND THE MOUNTAIN BOY †

One time some Government revenue agents went up in the mountains near North Wilkesboro to try and locate some

---

* H. Halpert, "Folktales and Jests from Delaware, Ohio," *Hoosier Folklore*, VII (1948), 72, gives another story in which a motorcycle is thought to be an animal.

† Botkin, p. 124, reprints a version of this story from Boyce House, *I Give You Texas*, p. 24.

stills they heard two mountain brothers were operating. They reached the cabin of one of the brothers, but there was nobody at home except the mountain man's twelve-year-old son.

The revenue agents asked the boy where his father and uncle were, and he replied, "They're just over the hill."

"Well," replied the revenue agents, "we'll give you fifteen dollars to take us over the hill where they are, when we come back."

"Naw," replied the boy. "You gimme the fifteen dollars now, 'cause if you go over the hill you ain't comin' back."

JES' PLOWED OFF

During World War II, Governor J. Melvin Broughton was up in the hindmost part of an extreme western North Carolina county selling victory bonds. Sighting a mountaineer in a field, directing a plow attached to a mule, the governor approached him. "Good morning, sir, I'm Governor Broughton of your state."

"Never heard tell of ye," was the rejoinder.

"Ever heard of President Roosevelt and Mr. Churchill?" said the governor. The mountaineer shook his head.

"Ever heard of Pearl Harbor?" said the governor.

"Naw, I ain't never heard tell of her neither," said the plowman.

"Well," said the governor, "I'm selling victory bonds so we can win the war for President Roosevelt and Mr. Churchill, and avenge Pearl Harbor."

"Giddap," said the plowman to his mule, leaving the governor standing there at the other end of the field.

The farmer's wife was waiting for him with a drink of

water at the other end of the field. When he got to where she was waiting for him, she said, "Who's that feller standing down at the other end of the field?"

"Some feller by the name of Broughton," replied the plowman. "He's got a friend named Roosevelt, who got in a mess with a gal named Pearl Harbor, over on Church Hill, and he asked me to sign his bond. So I jes' plowed off."

THE NEGRO COUNTERFEITER AND
THE WHITE MOUNTAIN STOREKEEPER

One time some colored fellows who made bad money made a error, an' stid of de machine makin' ten-dollar bills dey made some nine-dollar bills.

Dey hate to work in vain; so dey holds a confunce an' try an' figger out how dey gonna spend dese nine-dollar bills. Finally, after dey done talk to an' fro, dey settles on what de bestes' way to spend de nine-dollar bills. Dey figger dat it's bes' for one of 'em to go up in de mountains an' pass 'em off on mountain people.

So one of 'em makes his way up to Marshall an' goes in a mountain man's li'l store an' buys a dime's worth of cheese, an' han's him one of dese nine-dollar bills.

De mountain man takes it an' gives him his change. Den de colored fellow buys a box of sardines an' han's de mountain man 'nother nine-dollar bill. De mountain man, jus' like befo', takes de bill an' gives de colored fellow de change.

De colored fellow say to hisse'f, "I sho done come to de right place to pass dese bills." So he takes out 'nother nine-dollar bill an' say, "You seems to have a lot of change, frien', so I'd sho lack for you to gimme change for dis bill, too." So dis here time de mountain man reched over in de cigar box where he stacked his money an' give de colored fellow three three-dollar bills for de nine de colored fellow done give him.

Ghost Stories and Prophecy

THE STUBBORN PIANO *

Right after slavery time was over there was an old man who lived alone after his wife done died. While his wife was livin' she always liked to play a piano she had in her front-room. So just before she died she called the old man to her bedside and asked him never to sell or move the piano out of the house, 'cause she loved it so much.

A little later on, however, the old man got tired of livin' on such a big farm. So he sold this place and bought him a smaller farm. The following day he started moving his furniture and other things out of the house, but when he tried to move his wife's piano it would turn around and go back into the room he had taken it from. Every time he'd get the piano to the front door it would turn right around and go back into the room where his wife used to play it.

The old man was so disgusted that he offered a large sum of money to anyone who could move the piano out of the house. During this time "root women" were very popular. So a colored root woman heard about the old man's offer and went to see him. She told him that if she couldn't move the piano out of the house she'd die and go to hell "ballin' the jack." So the old man told the root woman to go home and get her roots and come back and see what she could do.

---

* Louis C. Jones, "The Ghosts of New York: An Analytical Study," *Journal of American Folklore*, LVII (1944), 245, mentions similar ghostly powers and activities. Cf. Motif E236.4. "Return from the dead because last will was not fulfilled."

When the root woman returned, she brought her mother with her. The root woman's mother was frightened about what the root woman had said to the old man, and tried to persuade her daughter not to try and move the piano, saying that she had heard of people makin' big promises and sayin' what they hoped would happen to 'em if they couldn't do a job, and then havin' things happen to 'em that they said would happen if they didn't do what they done said they could do.

But the root woman wouldn't listen to her mother; she took out her roots and started tryin' to move the piano out of the house. But the piano did just as it had done before; it moved out of the room it was in, but when it got to the front door leadin' out to the front porch, it turned around and went back into the room where it stood all the time. On its way back to the room, it knocked the root woman down and killed her so the root woman with her roots died, and everybody says they believe that she is in hell, ballin' the jack.

THE TAXICAB DRIVER AND THE GIRL GHOST *

Mr. Ramseur, a taxicab driver in the great metropolis of Charlotte, tells me that one afternoon he was hailed by an unremarkable young girl who climbed into his cab and gave him the address of a residence in the city to take her to. Mr. Ramseur proceeded to take her there. While they were rid-

---

* This legend, listed by Baughman as Motif E332.3.3.1. "The Vanishing Hitchhiker," has probably been collected more frequently than any other folktale in the United States. In a series of articles, R. K. Beardsley and R. Hankey, "The Vanishing Hitchhiker," *California Folklore Quarterly*, I (1942), 303-335; "A History of the Vanishing Hitchhiker," *California Folklore Quarterly*, II (1943), 13-

ing along nothing was said, and pretty soon they had arrived at the address. But at that time the strangest thing happened. When Mr. Ramseur got out to open the door for the girl and collect his fare, there was no one there. Mr. Ramseur was astonished. He knew the girl hadn't gotten out of the car anywhere, but he finally collected himself well enough to go up and ring the doorbell of the address the mystery girl had given him.

An elderly lady came to the door. Mr. Ramseur told her of his dilemma, and she looked a little startled as she said, "Mr. Ramseur, this is not the first time this has happened. The girl that you just described to me was my daughter, and she was killed by an automobile on her way home, on the very same corner that you picked up that girl on, three years ago. At least four or five other people have come and told me the same story you have told me." So Mr. Ramseur thanked the lady, but refused to accept the cab fare she offered him.

THE MASTER'S LAST DAY TO FEED THE HOGS

This is a story my father used to tell about his never getting a whippin' when he was a little slave boy. Papa said that one mornin' his old master took him out with him to feed his hogs without lettin' his mistress know he'd took papa with him. Seems like papa's old master always let his

---

26; Louis C. Jones, "Hitchhiking Ghosts in New York," *California Folklore Quarterly*, III (1944), 289-292, over one hundred versions from the United States and a few from other countries are cited. Since the publication of these articles, further numbers have been recorded. The Indiana University Folklore Archives, for instance, contains fifty-seven unpublished versions of the story collected, for the most part, from college students in Michigan and Indiana.

wife know when he was takin' Silas off of the premises, but this particular mornin' he took papa along with him without lettin' her know.

Papa said that his old master had about nine different hog-pens, and that he had a different whoop [hog-call] for every one of 'em, and that that mornin' as he went 'roun' to the pens he'd go in the pen, and talk to the hogs, and say, "Now (callin 'em by names), now Blackie," and so on, "This is the las' mornin' I's gonna feed you. Silas, here, gonna feed you from now on." So papa said after him and his old master done fed all the pigs in nine hog-pens that they went on back to the house, an' the old master went on upstairs to his bedroom. Papa went on out to the wood-pile to bring in some stovewood, and while he was pickin' it up his old mistress comed out with a bullwhip and ask him where he been all the mornin', and she couldn't find him. He told her, "Please don't whip him, 'cause she ain't never had no cause to whip him," and that "old master done took him to feed the hogs. That's the why that he ain't been on the premises that mornin', and that if'n she 'low him to go upstairs and see the master he can prove his whereabouts." So the old mistress tell him to come on and go back to the house with her to the old master's room upstairs, and bring him down to prove what he say. So papa follow her on into the house, and go upstairs to the old master's bedroom and walk in. He call the old master, but he don't answer; so finally papa goes to the bed what the old master layin' on, and he ain't breathin'—he dead. So papa run down the stairs and tell the old mistress that the old master dead. So she thowed the bull whip down and runned up the stairs fast as she can carry herself. She find the old master dead sho nuff. After this, papa feed the hogs ever mornin', like the old master done told the hogs he was goin' to do, and papa never was threaten with no whippings no mo'.

Tall Tales

THE WOMAN HURRICANE *

Many a storm swooped down on Wilmin'ton and nailed it good, dat dey has, but de one dat give it a catchin' in de side de worstes' was dat woman hurricane dey call Hazel. Dat Hazel sho did nail Wilmin'ton good—didn't take jes' one whop at de town—it took two, dat it did. De first time it blowed in it tore de roof offen our house, blowed down de walls an' de ceilins, an' if'n me an' my mama an' papa an' little six-years-old brother hadn't a runned outen de house an' falled down on de ground, an' laid dere till de storm done gone on 'bout its neverminds, we'd all been kilt, dat we would. It come putty near washin' us out, but it jes' played aroun' wid a old man's house what lived pieceways down de road fum us, dat it did. De first time it hit it took de old man's house wid it, and carried it way up de coast to James City, an' set it down. Den it turnt 'roun' an' comed back an' got de old man's horse what was tied to a tree in de yard an' carried him an' de tree in de yard up to James City, an' set him an' de tree down in de same yard where it done put de house in de first place, dat it did.

THE MYSTERIOUS HAND IN THE OCEAN †

There was a ship from Elizabeth City that was out in the water during the time the storm Diana went on a rampage.

* Baughman lists parallel stories under Motifs X1611.3.8. (a) "Wind blows house" and X1611.3.8. (e) "Wind blows trees."

† Cf. Motif F420.5.1.1. "Water-spirits save shipwrecked people."

94

The boat was completely destroyed. It had a crew of seven white men and two Negroes, and out of that number only the captain could swim. So they all gave themselves up as lost as the boat capsized and they were hurled into the water. Imagine their great surprise, then, when a giant hand came up out of the water and held them all in it until help arrived. The strange thing about the whole matter is that at the spot where the boat went down there is no sign of land at all; it is said to be bottomless. But there was no sign of the remains of the boat either, when the storm was over. The entire crew was saved.

This is one of the most talked-of mysteries in Pasquotunk County.

THE ARREST OF THE TWO-YEAR-OLD

De Mocksville Picnic is big doin's ever year. Look like policemans just hangin' 'roun' waitin' for de time to come when de Mocksville Picnic roll 'roun' so dey can 'rest a lots o' colored people an' put 'em to jail an' make 'em some money.

Dey makes a whole lots of 'rests ever year, but de worse one I done ever seen was las' year. A man's little two-year-old baby boy what been eatin' too many hamburgers an' drinkin' too many coca-colas took sick, an' was vomitin' all over de groun', an' wobblin' from side to side. A policeman seed de li'l fellow an' come up an' 'rested him for bein' drunk. But dat ain't all; he 'rested his papa for aidin' an' abettin'.

BOB BENFIELD AND THE BEAR *

Tell tale about a man named Bob Benfield. Bob Benfield say he gone out pickin' blackberries one day when a big black bear gets after him. He say he run an' run till he come to a mill pond froze over. He say he run out 'cross de ice wid de bear close in 'hin' 'im. But de bear be so heavy, an' de ice so thin, till he break through an' never ketch up wid Bob Benfield.

A man what listenin' to Bob say he don't b'lieve de tale; so he ask Bob how he be pickin' blackberries at de same time de water in de pond was froze over. So Bob haf to tell 'nother tale. He tell de man dat de bear be runnin' him from July till Christmas.

THE TOBACCO MILLIONAIRES' SONS' CHRISTMAS GIFTS

One Christmas two little boys, sons of tobacco kings, were discussin' what their papas give 'em for Christmas. The first one said, "My father give me a tobacco plantation, a tobacco warehouse, and a tobacco factory for Christmas. What did your father give you?"

---

* This tall tale is fairly common in the United States. It is listed by Baughman as Motif X1133.2. "Man escapes from bear by running for a long time, from summer to winter." Baughman cites *Hoosier Tall Stories*, The Federal Writers' Project, 1937, p. 8; H. Halpert, "Folktales and Jests from Delaware, Ohio," *Hoosier Folklore*, VII (1948), 69; A. P. Hudson, *Humor of the Old Deep South* (New York, 1936), pp. 171-172; V. Randolph, *Funny Stories About Hillbillies* (Girard, Kansas, 1944), p. 11; *Joe Allen's Fireside Tales* (New Bedford, Mass., 1941), pp. 13-14.

"Oh!" replied the second little boy, "my father didn't give me nothin' but a toy train."

"Say he did?" replied the first little boy, who was visiting him. "Let's go in the house and see it."

"Oh no, I couldn't do that," replied the second little boy. "I'd like to, but I can't. You see, my father gave me the Southern Railroad."

Animal Tales

THE POLLY PARROT AND THE CHICKENS *

One time there was a colored man noted for stealin' chickens. He was livin' 'roun' Landis then, but he come from somewhere in Georgia. One night while walkin' down the road with a sack on his back he decided to stop by Mr. Charlie's chicken house and get him a sack full o' chickens. It was just about dusk dark, so he wasn't able to see exactly what he was gettin' and puttin' in the sack. He just grabbed up as many o' the fowls as he could take at one whop. He got an old parrot in the shuffle but didn't know it, 'cause the old parrot was wise, and didn't open his mouth the whole night long.

The next mornin' when the colored man started to town to sell the chickens he met Mr. Charlie.

Mr. Charlie said, "John, what you got in that sack?"

"Oh, that's just some potatoes I'm takin' to town to sell," said John.

Then the old parrot spoke up and said, "No it ain't, Mr. Charlie. He's got a sack o' your chickens, and he's got me all mixed up in here with 'em."

---

* Cf. Motifs K427. "Clever animal betrays thief" and B211.3.4. "Speaking parrot."

WHY I LEFT GEORGIA *

I had no mother and father when I was nine years old; so I went to live with my uncle and aunt in Jasper County, Georgia.

One day my uncle sent me with a note to one of his neighbors who lived about two miles from our house. I had to cross fields and woods in order to get to the neighbor's house. First there would be a field, and then a stretch of woods.

When I went through the woods I was scared, because the trees were so thick until it looked like it was dark all the time. But I made it over to my uncle's neighbor's house and delivered the note without seeing anything, and without hearing anything. But when I got halfway back to my uncle's house I suddenly heard a whistle. I wondered who could be whistling at me out there in the woods, so I stopped and looked around in all directions, but I didn't see nobody. I started walking toward my uncle's house again, but I hadn't gone very far when I heard the whistle again.

This time I turned around and looked good in the direction from which the whistle came, and—to my great horror and surprise—I saw a coach-whip snake standing straight up and whistling. I was so frightened I didn't know what to do. I started running towards my uncle's house, the snake

* Beliefs about coach-whip snakes are common among Southern Negroes and whites alike. Closely parallel texts are given in N. I. White, ed., *The Frank C. Brown Collection of North Carolina Folklore*, I (Durham, 1952), p. 637; J. K. Strecker, "Reptile Myths in Northwestern Louisiana," *Publications of the Texas Folklore Society*, IV (1925), 50-51; C. J. Milling, "Is the Serpent Tale an Indian Survival?" *Southern Folklore Quarterly*, I (1937), 144-145.

right in behind me. Finally I gave out and had to stop and rest. When I stopped to rest the snake caught up with me and stood up straight again and whistled. I was so frightened that I looked the snake straight in the eye without batting an eyelid.

I must have charmed him instead of him charming me, because pretty soon he stretched hisself out on the ground again, stopped whistling, and passed by me without harming me and went on into an adjoining field. I then ran on home scared out of my wits.

My aunt and uncle were not at home when I got there, so I got a writing tablet, a pencil, and an envelope and wrote my grandmother in Salisbury to send for me, telling her that I wanted to come and live with her. She wrote back and told my aunt and uncle to get me ready and send me to live with her. My uncle and aunt wondered why I wanted to leave, but they got me ready and sent me on to my grandmother's anyway. I never told the reason for my leaving Georgia until ten years later when I had reached the age of nineteen and went back to visit them. Now I tell everybody why I left Georgia.

THE MOUNTAIN RAT WHO OUTWITTED THE CAT *

One time up in Wilkes County where you're likely to see a barrel of whiskey any place, any time, a little mouse fell into a barrel of mash and was strugglin' around tryin' to

---

* Five versions of this story, all from Negro informants, have been previously collected: Bacon and Parsons, "Elizabeth City County," p. 279; Parsons, *Sea Islands*; and Dorson, *Michigan*, pp. 40-41, 200. The story is perhaps a special form of Type 122H, "Wait Until I Get Dry."

swim out. No matter how hard he tried to get out, however, he was not able to do so. When he had almost given up hope of bein' saved he heard the footsteps of a cat outside of the barrel. So he started squeakin' to attract the attention of the cat. The cat heard him squeakin' and climbed up on the rim of the barrel and saw him strugglin' around in the whiskey tryin' to get out. When the rat saw the cat he said, "Please help me out of this barrel. If you save my life, I'll let you eat me when I dry off." So the cat reached down in the barrel with his claws, pulled the rat out of the barrel, and placed him on the ground to dry.

The cat did not watch the rat very closely after placing him on the ground; so when the rat was dry he crawled into his hole nearby and said, "Squeak, squeak." When the cat looked around and saw the rat in his hole with his head stickin' out, he yelled, "Say, fellow, I thought you said I could eat you when you got dry, if I saved your life."

"Oh! I'm likely to have said anythin' then," replied the mouse; "I was in my liquor then, and I'm likely to say anythin' when I'm in my liquor."

THE MOUNTAIN MAN AND THE PARROT *

One time a mountain man drove into North Wilkesboro with a load of wood to sell. He was hollerin' out about him havin' some wood for sale, when all at once he heard a

---

* This tale, which may be referred to Motif B211.3.4., "Talking parrot," has been previously collected at least twice. See Veronica Huss and Evelyn Werner, "The Conches of Riviera, Florida," *Southern Folklore Quarterly*, IV (1940), 143-144; Dorson, *Pine Bluff*, p. 42. Dorson's informant insisted that the incident of the parrot calling to the man delivering wood actually occurred in Pine Bluff, Arkansas.

voice say, "Throw it off, throw it off." So he drove up to
the yard where he thought he'd heard the voice say, "Throw
it off," and unloaded the wood. When he had unloaded all
of the wood he went up to the door of the house and
knocked on it. A colored woman who lived there came to
the door, and the mountain man said, "That'll be four
dollars for the load of wood you told me to throw off."

"What load of wood?" said the woman. "I ain't told
you to throw off no load of wood."

"Yes you did, by cracky," said the mountain man. "I
heered you tell me to throw it off."

"Naw you didn't neither," said the woman. "That musta
been my old parrot in the cage out there in the yard, 'cause
I ain't told you to throw off nothin'." And sure enough,
when the mountain man looked around there was the old
parrot out there in the yard, with his head hangin' down,
lookin' guilty.

Tales about Race

UNCLE JIM SPEAKS HIS MIND

A white preacher was preaching to a group of slaves one night, and he was talking about the gates of gold that the white folks would walk through, and the streets of silver and gold that they would walk on. He stopped and said, "Now you darkies need not worry, for God has some mighty good asphalt streets and some cement streets for you all to walk on." When he finished preaching about where the white folks would walk, he called on Uncle Jim, a very old slave, to lead the congregation in prayer. So Old Jim got down on his knees and said in a feeble voice, "Lord, I heared de preacher talking about where de white folks would walk, and us poor slaves would walk, but Lord, I done come up like de bulrushes wid my head bowed down, like de rushes covered wid de morning dew. Lawd, I knows dat I's your child and when I get to heaven I's gonna walk any damn where I please."

IF GOD BE FOR US

Way back almos' far as I can remember, dere was a old-timey preacher what take for his "talk about" one Sunday mornin' "If God Be For Us, Who Can Be Against Us?"

Ever time he'd have a say he'd end it up by sayin', "If God be for us, who can be against us?"

He goes on dis here fashion 'bout a hour or two, talkin' 'bout "If'n God be for us, who can be against us?" It's a hot day in Augus', an' some o' de sistren an' brethren begin to get weary an' starts to noddin' dey heads.

One of de sister's eyes get so heavy 'til she dozes off to sleep. But she wakes up real quick when de preacher squall out louder'n ever befo', "I say if'n God be for us, who can be against us?" an' when de preacher say dis de sister what been 'sleep stan' up kinda like she in a transon or sump'n an' squall out, "Niggers, dat's who."

COLOR MAKES A BIG DIFFERENCE *

One time a colored fellow up at Lillington runned over a mule wid his car and killed it. So dey 'rested him an' brung him to trial. When de day for de trial come de judge put him on de stand an' say, "Is you guilty of killin' dis mule, or ain't you?" So de colored fellow say, "I's guilty."

"What kind o' mule was it you runned over?" say de judge, "a black mule, or a white mule?"

"It was a white mule," say de colored fellow.

"Well, if'n it was a white mule," say de judge, "you say, 'Mr. Mule'; don't you come callin' no white mule just another mule!"

---

* Botkin, pp. 76-77, reprints a story from Alan Lomax, "I Got the Blues," *Common Ground*, (Summer, 1948), No. 4, pp. 51-52, in which a Negro is forced to call a white mule "Mister Mule." Hughes and Bontemps, p. 503, give an account explaining that Southern Negroes dare not buy white beans.

WHO'S READY FOR WHO? *

One time dere was a good old man in Winston. Him an' his wife been married for forty years, an' den one day she die. So de old man send for his son what live in New York City to come live wid him so he won't get lonesome all by hisse'f. De son a good son, so he go 'long wid what his papa want an' come on back home to Winston to live wid 'im.

De boy lan's him a good job at de 'bacco factory right off; so he do all right for hisse'f. He ain't married noways; so it fit in good for him an' his papa to be livin' wid one nother. But durin' of de day his papa, what was a retired railroad man, gets lonesome. So he ask his son to see if'n he can't get him somethin' nother to do at de 'bacco factory. De son say, all right, he'll see what he can do. So he talk wid de boss-man, an' de boss-man say he can give his papa little somethin' to do. So de old man start to workin' at de

---

* Hughes and Bontemps, p. 508, reprint the same tale from an unknown source. It is interesting to note that the national sit-in movement was begun by four A. and T. College students on February 1, 1960, in Greensboro, North Carolina. The youth responsible for the action was formerly a busboy who worked in the kitchen at a Woolworth Department Store. One day he asked the woman who was managing the kitchen for a raise in salary, whereupon she replied, "I can get niggers for a dime a dozen." That afternoon when the youth drew his pay envelope he took two dimes out of the envelope and said, "Here, take these two dimes and buy you two dozen niggers, 'cause I'm quittin'.'" Later that evening he returned to the store with three of his schoolmates, sat down with them at the lunch counter, and ordered a meal. They were refused service. Many tales similar to "Who's Ready for Who" resulted from this incident.

'bacco factory, too. He like dis here fine, 'cause him an' his boy can be together durin' of de daytime.

Dey have a frien' what run a nice café not far from de factory, name de Little Red Hen Café. So ever day dey goes down to de Little Red Hen to eat dinner together. One day, howbesomever, while dey is on de way to de Little Red Hen to eat, dey looks up an' sees a sign on a white café what read like dis here: "Dis restaurant am integrated." So de boy say, "Papa, les' us go in here an' eat dinner today." "Dat awright wid me," say de papa. So dey goes on in de restaurant an' takes a seat at one of de tables. When dey done set down a waitress comed over to where dey was an' ask 'em what dey like to have for dinner, so de old man say, "I'd like to have a plate of collard greens an' chitlins."

"Sorry, but dat ain't on de Me and You," say de waitress.

"Well den," say de old man, "bring me a plate of back-bones an' dumplin's."

"Sorry," say de waitress, "but dat ain't on de Me and You neither."

"Den," say de old man, "bring me a plate of cracklin' bread, baked sweet potatoes, fatback, an' pinto beans."

"Sorry," replied de waitress, "but dat ain't on de Me an You neither."

"Well den," say de old man, "if'n y'all ain't got none of dat I don't want nothin'; y'all always 'roun' here talkin' 'bout we ain't ready for y'all yet, but it's t'other way 'roun'. Y'all ain't ready for us yet." Then, turnin' to his son, he say, "Come on, boy! Let's go on down to de Little Red Hen and eat."

THE BLIND MAN WHO CHANGED HIS SONG

Just after Jack Johnson done come to be de first colored man to be de worl's heavyweight champion by knockin' out Jim Jeffries, a colored blind man what lived in Monroe was walkin' down de street wid his cup in han' singin' a song 'bout Jack Johnson dat go lack dis:

Jack Johnson be de champion of de worl',
Jack Johnson be de champion of de worl',
Jack Johnson be de champion, Jack Johnson be de champion,
Jack Johnson be de champion of de worl'.

A white man was walkin' by, who didn't lack colored peoples, an' what was mad anyways 'bout a colored man bein' de champion of de worl', an' he heered de blind man singin' de song. So he walked up to him an' say, "What's dat you sayin', nigger?"

So de blind man was rail scared. So he say rail quick, "Dis here what I say, ain't you heered me?"

Oh blessed be de name of de Lord,
Oh blessed be de name of de Lord,
Oh! blessed be de name, blessed be de name,
Blessed be de name of de Lord.

THE SMART MOCKSVILLE NEGRO

One time at Salisbury they decided to integrate the post office on account of the mail rush at Christmastime. So they posted an examination, and college boys from all around came to take it.

A twenty-one-year-old Negro farm boy from Mocksville heard about the examination they were giving to those who wanted to qualify for the work. So he walked in to Salisbury the day the examination was scheduled to be given. He wore bright green trousers and a yellow shirt with a red bow tie. When he reached the examination room he was given an examination sheet along with all the college students.

The examination was a multiple-choice test where you underlined one of the four possible answers that you thought to be correct. The examination was supposed to last for an hour and a half, but the Mocksville Negro finished the examination in twenty minutes. When he had finished, he took his paper and handed it to the examiner.

The examiner was amazed at his speed, and was more amazed when he discovered that the Negro had missed only one question and had made a grade of 95. So he told the Negro to follow him down to the mail room, that he wanted him to start to work immediately. He put the Negro to sorting mail, and the Negro started to throwing the mail in the pigeon holes so fast that the examiner could hardly believe his eyes. "My, how fast you work," he said.

"Humph! That ain't nothin'," said the Negro. "I'd work a lots faster'n that if'n I could read."

BIG JOHN AND LITTLE JOHN *

One time durin' slavery time a slave master from Georgia named Master Charlie bet a slave master from North Caro-

* The general story of the contest between two slaves arranged by their masters is treated by Dorson, *Michigan*, pp. 55-56 and 210. Brewer, in his earlier collection, "Juneteenth," pp. 50-51, gives a Texas tale of a similar contest. Brewer's North Carolina story, however, contains a special element, Type 1085, "Pushing a Hole

lina named Master Jim that the baddest slave he had could whip the baddest slave he had. So they set a date for a fight between 'em, and decided the slave master from Georgia would bring his slave to North Carolina on that date to fight the North Carolina slave master's slave. The slave master from Georgia's slave was a great big six-footer with large muscles called Big John, while the slave master from North Carolina's slave was a little short thin man about five feet tall; they called him Little John. He'd been whippin' all the other slaves, 'cause he was a good rastler.

The night before the fight was to be, the slave master from Georgia got to the place where the fight was being held with Big John, and tied him to a big tree in the woods. Little John heard Big John was there, so he went down to the place where Big John was tied to the tree and stayed there all scared to death. Just as the sun was risin', one of the slaves come and untied Big John, and took him to get a drink of water.

Little John had been wonderin' how he was gonna whip Big John. So when the slave took Big John to get a drink of water, Little John thought of somethin' that he might do that would cause him to win the fight. So he went to the tree that Big John had been tied to, cut the bark off of it in front, and took out an ax and cut a big hole all the way through the tree. Then he picked up the bark off of the ground and put it back over the hole he'd cut in the tree.

After he'd put the bark back where it was in the first

into a Tree." This story sometimes appears alone rather than as part of a longer tale. It is known in both Europe and Asia. Previously collected versions in the U.S. are Spanish-American, Juan B. Rael, *Cuentos Españoles de Colorado y de Nuevo Méjico* (Stanford University, n.d.), nos. 291, 292, and one American Indian version which was probably learned from French-American sources, F. G. Speck, "Penobscot Tales," *Journal of American Folklore,* XXVIII (1915), 55.

place, then he went up to his master's house, put on Master Jim's best suit, got one of his cigars, and told the stable boy to bring the buggy around front. Meanwhile, all the other slaves were down in the big field waitin' to see the big fight. Little John was already ten minutes late, and Big John's owner was braggin' about him bein' scared.

All at once they sighted a cloud of dust. Little John had the horses runnin' as fast as they could go. When he reached the field of battle he stopped the buggy, jumped out, and kissed Master Jim's wife. Then he walked over to the big tree where Big John was tied and hit it with his fist, and his fist went through the tree. Finally, he booted Master Jim in the seat of his pants.

At the sight of all of this Big John broke loose and started runnin'. When they finally caught Big John they asked him why he run. He said, "When I saw Little John kiss that white woman I got a little shaky. When he hit the tree my heart stopped beatin', but when he kicked that white man I had to go, for I knowed if that fellow would kiss a white woman in front of a white man, then kick a white man and he say nothin', Lawd have mercy, what would he do to me?"

THE FISH PEDDLER WHO CHANGED HIS TUNE

Used to be a ol' white man down to Wilmington what peddled fish ever Saddy mornin' in a colored part o' town. He had a special li'l tune he hollered all de time so de people can know he prowlin' 'roun' de neighborhood. He always say, "I got porgies, I got catfish, an' I got black bass."

He sell a lot o' fish too, what he have strung on a long pole so's dey could be seed an' you could pick out what somever fishes you wanted.

Everbody like de ol' man's fish, an' he have a sell-out most all de time.

One time, though, dere was a colored fellow what come to visit his sister dat live on one of de streets where de ol' fish peddler make his roun's, an' he hear de fish peddler hollerin' what kind o' fish he got an' think when de ol' peddler get to dat part what say "black bass" dat he sayin' a "black bastard." So he goes an' jumps on de ol' peddler an' gives him a good beatin'. All de same dis here didn't keep de ol' fish peddler from peddlin' his fish dat nex' comin' Saddy mornin' like as befo'. He jes' change de tune he holler.

When he comed roun' dat nex' comin' Saddy he say, "I got porgies, I got catfish"—an' den he point his finger at de spot where de black basses is hangin' on de pole an' say, "and I got some of dese, too."

THERE IS A REASON FOR EVERYTHING

One time a nigger what used to work for a white man met de white man on de street. He seed de white man had a fishin' pole slung cross his shoulder, so he say, "Mr. Charlie, is you goin' fishin'?

"Yes I is," say de white man.

"Well den," say de nigger, "since I ain't workin' today, how 'bout lettin' me go 'long with you an' tote de bait you got in dat bucket in yo' hand?"

"All right," replied de white man, "come on, and let's go." So de nigger grabbed de bucket with de bait in it and dey goes on down to de river.

Dey ain't down dere no time 'fo' de white man gets a bite, an' when he jerk his pole out of de river he had a seven-pound catfish on it. De nigger was so excited when he saw de fish till he started runnin' up and down de riverbank.

Not knowin' what he was doin, he falls in de river. De white man seed him fall in so he jumped in de water and saved him from drownin'.

De next day de white man was tellin' one of his good buddies dat he saved de nigger's life. "Is you done lose yo' mind?" say his frien'. "How come you take a chance on losing yo' life jest to save a nigger's life?"

"Well, it was like dis," say de white man. "De nigger had de bait!"

THE WHITE BOY WHO WANTED TO BE A NIGGER

One day a little white boy, whose father worked as a book-keeper in a big department store in Charlotte, shocked his father by saying, "Father, I want to be a nigger."

"Why do you want to be a nigger, son?" asked his father.

"So I can buy me a Cadillac," replied the little boy.

THE WHITE BOY WHO ACTED LIKE A NIGGER

One time a little white boy went to a county fair with his father. While there his father met a friend of his and started talking to him. The little boy, tiring of grown folks' conversation, wandered off to a soda-water stand and started buying coca-colas. Every time he'd buy a bottle of coca-cola, he'd take a penny out of his pocket and throw it away. He threw away quite a few pennies but did not know his father was watching him throw 'em away.

When his father finished talking with his friend he walked over to the stand where the little boy was buying the coca-colas and said, "Son, why are you buying so many sodas?"

"I'm actin' like a nigger, daddy," replied the boy.

"What do you mean, actin' like a nigger?" his father asked.

"Drinkin' too much, and throwin' money away," replied the boy.

THE COTTON-PICKIN' MONKEYS

I know this story is an out-and-out lie, and it was never told for the truth. Like a lot of folk tales, it was created only to entertain, and I wish that the good old Dr. Brewer could have heard it as I did, from the daddy rabbit of all Negro storytellers, Harrison Neal. This is how Neal told the story.

Way back 'fo' dey built de dam at de narrows, or de Badin pot rooms, likewise, I bound it must of been 'bout de time de gold mines was goin' full blast, an' long 'fo' my papa was kilt in de old Randolph mine, dey was a old Confed'rate granpappy what done lived to be a real ol' man an' had lots of money an' goods in de worl'. Fack, he 'bout de richest man in all dat neck o' de woods 'roun' Anson County.

When de ol' granpappy been a young man he lef' de plantation an' went an' fit in de war wid de Yankees, an' he did a real jam-up job o' fightin', too, from de fus' to de las'. But when he see de Confed'rates was whipped he lit out for home jes' like Moody's goose, an' got home in time to put in a good crop o' cotton an' tobacco. He ain't poke aroun' none. I bound he make dat dirt fly mo' samer'n a dog when he dig out a rat outen de dirt. De ol' man have a heaps o' luck wid his crops, an' de Lord bless him real good, 'cause when he pay off de croppers what hope him he have about two pots o' money lef'. Dat give him a good start. Fack is, he have a runnin' start, an' dat's de way he go atter things de rest o' his natural-born days. Seem like I heerd dat he married 'fo' de war, an' dat he first an' only chap was born de year dat he git home atter de war. Well sir, de ol' granpappy's wife she up an' die de year atter dat, an de ol' granpappy have to raise de boy by hese'f. I ain't never in no wise know what de boy's name been, but when he come to be 'bout twenty-one years old he marry up wid a gal what live in dem parts an' dey have a boy chile. 'Twasn't long atter dis 'fo' a runaway team kilt de ol' man's boy an' de yaller fever kilt his wife de nex' year. Dis leave just de ol' granpappy here to take care o' de granbaby an' raise him.

With all de farms, plantations, saw-mills, town property, an' two banks dat de old man own, he ain't got but dis one granbaby. Dat's de most onlies' blood-kin he got in de whole wide worl', so he love him more dan all de rest o' de worl', even he ownse'f. So he set out to do de granchile right. He give him whatsomever he heart desire, but de ol' granpappy ain't spoil de chile. He learn him real good, an' he make him hew to de line; so de boy come to be one o' de smartes' young men in dat neck o' de woods. Wid de ol' man bein' so freehearted wid de boy, it ain't in no shape changed his way of bein' stingy wid everybody else. He been more tighter dan de bark on a hick'ry tree. One day, howbesomever, late in de summer time atter all de crops been laid by, de ol' granpappy call he little granchile to him an' talk like unto dis here: "It's 'bout time now dat you go off somewhere to school an' learn 'bout how de rest o' de worl' live, 'cause you done learnt all dat dere be to be learnt 'roun' here."

So, long 'fo' de Jack Frost done make de 'simmons fall, de boy done trace his foosteps outen Anson County well on de way long de road to learnin' 'bout de rest o' de worl'. I boun' he learn real good, too, 'cause in roun' 'bout four years he done know all dey is to know in de school where de old man sent him. He have a handful o' know-how, an' know-who, an' wid dis he do real a sho-nuff good job. He work way off yonder in Souf Ameriky, but he job don't in no wise trouble de boy.

So he have a lot of time on he hands, but wid all de know-how he got he ain't fergit 'bout what he done learnt on he granpappy farm. He kinda took up wid dat farm life. So he 'cides to show de people down dere how to grow cotton, an' he puts in 'bout a hundred acres of cotton.

Now, de granson, he right smart 'bout learnin' dumb brutes how to do sumpin' nother. He done trained many a dog on he granpáppy's plantation, an' when he had a mind to he broke in all de saddle horses for his granpappy. So atter de cotton done growed up an ' de bolls done opened up, an' dey ain't nobody in dem parts what knows how to pick cotton, de granson 'cides dat he gonna get him some monkeys an' learn 'em to pick it, an' he do just dat. He gets him two pet monkeys an' learn 'em how to pick cotton. Dey works so fas' dat ain't no time 'fo' de crop on de whole hundred acres done been gathered. De boy so proud o' de monkeys dat he writ his ol' granpappy an' tell him 'bout how fas' de monkeys can pick cotton.

De ol' man gets de letter what he granchile done writ him 'bout his trainin' de cotton-pickin' monkeys, an' he real proud o' what de boy done do, but he don't have no 'tickler interest in no monkey business. But in de very nex' letter dat de boy write his granpappy he tell him dat he comin' home for a spell, an' dat he have a demonstration he want him to witness when he done reach dere. It be 'long 'bout cotton-pickin' time when de boy get dere, an' he done brung de two cotton-pickin' monkeys wid him in a big box wid an air-hole cut in it. De ol' granpappy looks at de monkeys an'

ask de boy how come he done brung de monkeys wid him?
De boy tell him dat de why he done brung 'em is dat he
got a proposition he wanna put to him dat'll make him mo'
richer'n what he already be. At de name of money de ol'
granpappy prick his years up mo' samer'n dan a mule what
done spy a mad dog, an' say, "Le's hear what de proposition
be, son."

So de boy say, "Granpappy, if'n you'll 'vance me ten
thousand dollars I'll go back to Souf Ameriky an' get some
Injuns to catch me some more monkeys, an' we kin plant
'bout five thousand acres o' cotton, an' I'll get about a
hundred monkeys an' give 'em de knowledge how to pick
cotton an' you make 'bout fifty pots full o' money, 'cause
it don't in no wise cost much money to feed an' house a
monkey."

De ol' granpappy say dat dat don't make no never-mind
'bout dat—dat he don't want to hurt he white an' colored
fieldhan's, 'cause dey is easy hurted anyhow. But de boy say,
"Granpappy, dey is easy hurted anyways; dey's used to bein'
hurt; so what do dey bein' hurted mean to you makin' fifty
pots full o' money?" De old granpappy don't like to say "no"
to de boy right off; so he say to make a big loan like dat he
have to take de matter up wid de board o' directors o' de
bank. De boy say dat so much de better, to have de board
o' directors come out to de farm an' witness for deyse'f de
demonstration, an' when dey sees what de monkeys can do
dey boun' to see de why for makin' him de loan o' ten
thousand dollars to buy de monkeys an' sen' 'em to his granpappy to pick de cotton he gonna raise, an' if'n de ol'
granpappy can get de board to come out to de farm de nex'
mornin' real early 'fo' breakfast he gonna put on a demonstration for dem to witness dat dey ain't never witness in all
dey born days de Lord done give 'em before.

So dat nex' comin' day, very early in de mornin' time 'fo'

breakfast, de board o' directors been out to ol' granpappy's farm to see de demonstration. But 'fo' de demonstration take off to a runnin' start, de ol' granpappy th'ows a big breakfast for de board o' directors. Dey has eight or nine platters o' ham an' eggs, a washpot full o' grits, two or three gallon o' red-eye gravy, twelve pans o' biscuits, an' a five-gallon crock o' de bes' peach preserves. An' to cap de climax dey has three washpots o' coffee to wash all dis food down wid. Atter dey done filled dey craws up wid all dis food, dey goes on down to de cotton field where de boy's gettin' de monkeys' middles tied to a pole what go up dey back; an' in front of dey faces, just in far nuff out so dey can't reach it, he have a great big banana danglin 'fore 'em from a string. Den he take de monkeys an' put 'em 'twix' two rows o' cotton, side by side, wid a cotton sack on dey back, an' starts 'em off to pickin' cotton. De monkeys want dat banana swingin' in front of dey little faces, so de hungrier dey gets de more faster dey walks, de more faster dey works de more cotton dey picks, an' de more de cotton fly. De board members' eyes almost pops out when dey see dat; an' dey 'low dat dis be de out-doin'est demonstration dey done ever witness. So right dere on de spot de board vote to lend de boy de ten thousand dollars to buy some monkeys an' send 'em back to he ol' granpappy's farm to pick cotton. But de ol' granpappy say, "No, no," dat he ain't gonna do no such a thing, an' de board dey ain't neither.

But de headknocker of de board confab wid de ol' granpappy lack dis: "You say 'no' an' dat boy bein' as he is your own flesh an' blood. If'n we's got confidence in him, you is bound to have it, too, 'cause you done raised him up an' give him most o' de know-how." But de ol' granpappy answer him dat it ain't de boy, an' it ain't de monkeys, but just de same de answer be "no."

"Den what is it?" de board wanna know. So de old granpappy say dat it be dem meddlin' damn Yankees, dat what it be. De board members all look 'sprised when dey hears dis, so de headknocker of de board say, "Dey ain't no Yankees dis side o' Washington."

De ol' granpappy 'low dat *he* know dat good as *he* do, but he answer to de proposition still be's "no."

But de headknocker of de board insist on havin' de knowledge to know where do de Yankees come in.

At dis here 'joinder de ol' granpappy riz up straight from his chair an' say, "Y'all doesn't know dem meddlin' damn Yankees like I does. Here's where dey comes in—it's just lack dis: Time we gets dem monkeys here, an' we gets to de place where we's makin' money out of 'em, dem meddlin' damn Yankees gonna come down here an' free ever one of 'em."

THE INDIAN WON

One time a Negro and an Indian got in an argument about which race had produced the greatest man, the Indian or the Negro.

The Indian was convinced that his race had produced the largest number of great men, and the Negro was certain that *his* race had. So they decided to start naming the great men each race had produced. The agreement was that the Indian would name a great American Indian, and then the Negro would name a great American Negro. The Indian was to start naming the great men of his race first, so he said: "Tecumseh."

"Booker T. Washington," said the Negro.

"Sitting Bull," said the Indian.

"Frederick Douglass," said the Negro.

"Powhatan," said the Indian.

"Crispus Attucks," said the Negro.

An so they continued for about an hour, one man naming a great Indian and the other a famous Negro.

Finally the Indian said, "Wait a minute. I have something that will prove the Indian is a greater race than the Negro."

"All right," replied the Negro. "What you got?"

"Have you ever heard of little boys playing cowboys and niggers?" said the Indian.

RACE BETTING *

The same day that the motorcade of cars comprising the funeral procession of the late Daddy Grace's remains left Charlotte on the way to New Jersey, a Negro chauffeur and

---

* As mentioned above, this text represents a remarkable combination of an ancient story and a modern one. The ancient story—that dealing with the contest as to which can throw highest—belongs to Type 1063A "Throwing Contest: Trickster Shouts." Of the versions of this story collected in the United States, the one closest to our text is that previously published by Brewer in "Juneteenth," pp. 50-51, in which the contest also involves throwing with a slingshot. The following versions all deal with a contest in throwing a hammer or some other heavy object: Smetzer, "Negro Folktales," pp. 52-53; South Carolina Folk Tales, pp. 80-81; Richard Chase, Grandfather Tales (Cambridge, 1948), pp. 92-93; Isabel Gordon Carter, "Mountain White Folk-Lore: Tales from the Southern Blue Ridge," Journal of American Folklore, XXXVIII (1925), 353; Hurston, pp. 197-198; E. C. Parsons, "Folk-Tales Collected at Miami, Florida," Journal of American Folklore, XXX (1917), 223; Fauset, "Negro Folk Tales from the South," p. 250; Dorson, Michigan, pp. 162, 210. All but two of the above versions were collected from Negroes. The second half of our text, the story dealing with the bet on the number of Cadillacs, I have found in no other sources. Many tales similar to "Race Betting" were invented and circulated immediately after the death of Bishop Charles Manuel "Sweet Daddy" Grace on January 12, 1960. Bishop Grace had founded the House of Prayer for All People in Charlotte in 1926.

his employer, from Louisiana, who were on exceptionally cordial terms at all times, stopped in the vicinity where Daddy Grace's Charlotte House of Prayer was located.

They had got out of the car and were standing on a corner waiting for the cars to pass when they spied a little boy with a slingshot. "You know something," said the Negro's employer, who liked to play pranks on his chauffeur, "I'll bet I can throw higher than you can throw with a sling shot."

"I'll bet you can't," said the Negro.

"Well, all right, let's borrow that little boy's slingshot and see who can throw the highest. The one who throws the highest will have to pay the other five dollars."

"All right," said the Negro chauffeur, "that's a bet. You go on and throw first."

The white man took the slingshot from the little boy, put a rock in it, wound up, and threw it into the sky. One minute, two minutes, three minutes, four minutes, five minutes passed before the rock fell to the ground.

The Negro was at a loss to know what to do now, because he had no idea that his boss could throw a rock as high as he could. At any rate he took up the slingshot, put a rock in it, and started twirling the slingshot around and around, repeating at the same time, "John, get out of the way! Peter, get out of the way! Gabriel, get out of the way! Moses, get out of the way! Noah, get out of the way!" And when he said this the white man grabbed him by the arm and said, "Wait a minute, Here's your five dollars. Put that slingshot down before you knock the hell out of God."

But the Negro's employer was not through betting yet. He turned to his chauffeur and said, "Let's make another bet. Let's stand here on the corner a while and watch the cars go by. I'll bet you that Negroes own more Cadillacs than whites. So I tell you what let's do: for every white man that drives a Cadillac past here I'll give you a dollar, and for every colored man that drives a Cadillac past here you give me a dollar."

"All right," replied the Negro. "Let's get started." So they began to watch the cars that passed.

The first Cadillac that passed was driven by a Negro; soon another Cadillac passed, and it too was driven by a Negro. Then all at once Daddy Grace's funeral motorcade leaving Charlotte for New Jersey passed, and every car in it, fifty in all, was a Cadillac. The Negro was so disgusted he didn't know what to do. He took out his purse and started counting out one-dollar bills, saying to his boss, "Here, let me give you these fifty-three dollars rat now. That's the way it is with' niggers—they'd rather die and go to hell than see another colored man make some money."

BEING EQUALS DOESN'T ALWAYS PAY OFF

Shortly after the Negro sit-in demonstration in Greensboro, a white man who lived there and prided himself on practicing Christianity and treating his fellowman fair regardless of the color of his skin, started driving to Raleigh one morning on a business trip.

He had gotten about ten miles out on the highway when he saw a Negro man walking towards Raleigh. When he reached the spot on the highway where the Negro was, he stopped his car and invited the Negro to get in. The Negro thanked him and started to open the back door of the car and get in, but the white man stopped him and said, "Don't sit back there; come on up here in the front seat and sit by me. You're as good as I am." So the Negro said, "Thank you, sir," and climbed up in the seat beside him.

A little later on, the white man drove over into a clump of woods near the highway, took out his thermos bottle with ice water in it, and took him a drink. He then handed it to the Negro, and said, "Have a drink!" But the Negro said, "Thank you, sir, but I'll wait until we get to the next town and get me a paper cup to drink out of."

"Oh, that's all right," replied the white man. "Just turn the bottle up and drink out of the mouth of it. You're as good as I am."

Then the white man started up his car, but he had not gone more than 400 yards before he had a blowout and had to stop the car and drive it to one side of the road.

When he stopped the car both he and the Negro sat there looking at each other—one waiting for the other to say something. Finally the Negro broke the silence by saying, "Ain't it awful the fix we is in; just have to sit here and look at one 'nother, 'cause they ain't a nigger nowheres 'round to change this tire."

THE CHEROKEE INDIAN RESERVATION SOUP LINE

In the hills of North Carolina where the Great Smoky Mountains begin, there is a reservation for the Cherokee Indians controlled by the federal government.

Right after the First World War, during President Hoover's administration, when there were some really tough times and soup lines were being formed all over the country, a soup line was formed on this Cherokee reservation, where all the Cherokees and passers-by were served, except Negroes.

One time a hungry Negro passed through that section, got in line with the others, and waited to be served. In front of him were a Cherokee Indian, a Chinaman, and a Japanese.

There was a government man checking the nationality of all those passing through the soup line. When the Cherokee was asked his race, he replied, "Me Cherokee." When the Chinaman was asked his nationality, he replied, "Me Chinee." When the Japanese got to where the government man was and was asked his nationality, he replied, "Me Japanee." The Negro was next; so he walked over to where the man checking the races was standing, and when asked his nationality replied, "Me spookanee."

2

Folk Talk

*I'd rather be in New York starvin' to death
than to be down here with nothin' but Monday
mornin', meal, molasses, mules, an' meanness.*

The United States is one of those countries where environmental factors have caused the inhabitants to develop the habit of exchanging opinions in public places. People living in the United States enjoy expressing their opinons where they can be plainly heard by more than one person. Some of this talk is meaningless and foolish, but most of it is meaningful and sensible.

Until recently folk talk thrived, for the most part, in rural and isolated districts, but with the migration of farm and mountain folk to cities and towns, it has become almost as prevalent in urban centers as it was in rustic communities. City sidewalks and buses have replaced the old time liars' benches.

Because of its odd and picturesque qualities, Negro folk talk is one of the most interesting branches of American folk talk. The most fascinating Negro folk talk is found in the states of South Carolina and Louisiana, but North Carolina Negroes also rate high, as these sayings will reveal.

General Aphorisms and Observations

My wife tells me that I talk too much. She says that if God had intended for me to talk so much He'd a give me two mouths and one ear, instead of two ears, an' one mouth.

Now I lay me down to sleep, a dollar down and a dollar a week—dat's de procedure.

Never mess wid a nigger when he's chawin' on a bone.

You let them run their mouths, and you run your business.

Nothin' the size of a rabbit can outrun a cow.

Some people tries to go 'roun' de worl' in a pea-pod boat.

If you can't keep up wid de bell cow, you have to gallop along wid de gang.

RABBIT PHILOSOPHY: Never trust a man; he might have a dog in his pocket.

It don't take no more time to put good paint on it than it do to put bad paint on it.

Evertime it rains it catches me with a fork. [With a fork: a knife is also needed if one is to eat properly, i.e., to do anything fully.]

ON COURTSHIP: I do like the baseball boys do—I hits and runs.

You might get by ol' man "need-more," but you sho can't get by ol' "have-to-have."

Colorful Turns and Figures of Speech

[Summer] kept on nippin' an' tuckin' till it got here.

It's hot nuff today to melt de harness offen a billy-goat.

Looks like we might have "fallin' weather" today; it kinda favors snow.

Dat weather man know what he talkin' 'bout most of de time. Science sho done walked up de road a long way, ain't it?

I's hoarse from singin' at de revival we had las' week ever night; I'm a strong warrior when hit comes to singin'.

Boy, I sho hopes you gonna invite me to dinner at yo' house again, 'cause yo' mama kin sho put a hurtin' on dem beans.

I done noticed the sky time and time again, an' ain't as blue as it used to be way back in my comin' up. I done threaded many a needle by de moonlight.

A. I drove de hound out of dat car.
B. She made de hound out of dat dress.
C. He beat de hound out of dat nigger.

He think dat S-T-O-P mean State Tax On Peanuts.

TO A VERY YOUNG FATHER: You strowed your mess early, didn't you?

I'm gonna git all o' my things out o' dis pocketbook rat now. I got a li'l eight-year-ol' girl at home, an' she lack to ramshack thu my pocketbook all de time.

I'm goin' do to one of dem way-back-in-de country dances an' raise me five dollars worth of hell.

Religion and Faith

If God tells you to take one step, take two.

He's a sho-nuff, stomp-down devil-chasin' preacher.

People goin' 'roun' here talkin' 'bout dey gonna build "shelter" houses to keep de bombs offen 'em if'n dey ever drops one here in Salisbury. I ain't thinkin' 'bout buildin' none, 'cause God's my shelter. I keeps my mind straight on God an' my head right on his shoulder. I knows God, an' God knows me, an' I talks to God, an' God talks to me. I gets my consolation from Daniel when de lion done turnt on him in de den, an' Daniel pray to de Lawd an' ask him to come down an' save him from de lion's jaws. So God hears Daniel an' say, "I hears my chillun down dere cryin' for help, so I got to go down dere an' loose 'em." God gonna look after you if'n you trusts Him an' do what he say do. Dat's fair, ain't it? 'Cause look a-here, if you go down here an' gets you a job, don't you do what de man say do what you work for if'n you want to be paid off? So dat's just de way it be wid God; if you wants God to pay off you got to do what he say. I got my shelter—GOD.

The higher up you go in life, the closer you have to walk with God.

EULOGIZING A DEAD CHURCH SISTER: I don't know where she are, but wherever she are, she are.

Dese preachers dese days can't tell you everthing from de pulpit; dey's gonna die rotten like de sweet potato. ["Rotten like de sweet potato": without being of use to anybody.]

You know dat tall skinny rawboneded man what used to change tires down to de Frog Pond filling station? Well, dey tells me somebody throwed for him 'las' Saddy, an' he started throwin' up frogs an' lizards an' snakes las' night, an' went into a spasm an' died. ["Throwed for him": cast a spell on him, voodooed him.]

Current Events and Race Relations

All dis land as far as you can see belonged to fifty-cents-a-day men. Now dat white man what owns de land is a hundred-dollars-a-day man.

I lived in Faith seventeen years—me and another colored man—just the two of us colored people, an' I ain't never see no sign, NIGGER READ AND RUN. I read ever day of them seventeen years I was there, but I never did run.

Dem folks up de road [in Northern cities, specifically New York] gives away what de folks down here goes up town an' buy.

New York'd be all right, but dey's so many Southern niggers up dere eatin' watermelons till de rinds is floatin' all down 135th street, an' stoppin' de traffic.

What was the use of the Yankees freein' us, if we wasn't gonna do nothin'?

God don't have no respect of person; the Devil's the one running this color business.

ON WHITE SEGREGATIONISTS: Dey don't wanna give up de old landmark.

AN ELECTION DAY REMARK ON SENATOR GOLDWATER: He put a bad mouth on hisse'f to start wid; now he tryin' to take it all back.

If'n Goldwater get 'lected in '64 we gonna have col' water in '65, an' no water in '66.

Behavior and Etiquette

You see I started off de day on de wrong foot—if I had done what I started to do at first—gone by de fillin' station an' got my car serviced first stid of goin' by de liquor store an' servicin' myself first—I wouldn't a had no wreck.

I was comin' down with a cold las' night, boy, but de minute I started to sneezin' I went an' poured me out a big swig o' noise in a glass an' drunk it, an' dis mornin' when I waked up I was fit as a fiddle. ["Noise": Strong drink of any kind.]

A. A nigger'd rather tell a lie on credit than tell the truth for cash.
B. A nigger'd rather tell a lie on another one than eat when he's hungry.

I ain't goin' up de road; I'm gonna stay right here on de old plant-ground.

I'm just a country boy; I done made brick in Balt'more an' coal mined in Pennsylvania, but I ain't never forgot my raisin'.

Ol' man Johnson I used to work wid down to de railroad shops brung his ol' heavy overcoat to work wid 'im ever day de Lord sent—winter an' summer, an' when you'd ast 'im how come he brung it wid 'im ever day, he'd say, "Well, I tells you; it's lack dis—it's better to have sumpin' an' don't need it dan it is to need sumpin' an' don't have it."

I always kept my head up and my dress down.

Ol' woman I works for come tryin' to curse me out in a roundabout way dis mornin'; she didn't think I knowed it, but I catched it on de first fly.

My boy says dat I'm at de bottom of de hill when it comes to knowin' right from wrong.

I went to work dis mornin', and I sho had myse'f some luck dis time; I got paid off an' laid off.

My son what used to be de janitor down to de courthouse finished up college in Hist'ry, but he couldn't get no job so it throwed him right back in de suds.

I don't care if dat ol' white woman I works for don't come an' git me an' carry me to work dis mornin'. I ain't got a chile or a chick—nothin' but de cats, and you knows what dey eats.

You can't take a man out of a ditch an' put a pencil behind his ear an' put him in an office; if'n you do you's sho gonna mess up.

I done told dat farm agent dat de bes' way to git rid of dem worms eatin' up dem 'mato vines is to put ashes on 'em. He got it de book-way, but dem worms don't know nothin' 'bout no book.

3

Superstitions

If your second toe is bigger than your big toe, you will rule your husband.

Although on the decline, one of the branches of North Carolina Negro folklore that still survives is superstitions. "Signs," as they are called by the great majority of Negroes, still play an important part in the daily life of the North Carolina Negro. Negro college students are a possible exception to this rule: many of them declare that they have no belief in superstitions at all, and this may be the cause of a substantial decrease in the number of superstitions quoted by North Carolina Negroes. But as of 1965, superstitions still play an important role in the North Carolina Negro adult's way of life.

Signs

To sneeze in the morning tells that misfortune is near you.

If your shoestring comes untied, somebody is talking about you.

If in stirring your tea the leaves or stalks keep in the middle of the cup, it is a sign that you will soon be married or talk to a stranger or an absent friend.

When bread or cake or pie burns in spite of you, your husband or lover is angry.

To forget to put coffee or tea in the pot is a sure sign that you will hear good news.

To awake in the morning on the right side is a sign of good luck.

If a slat falls out of a bed, it is a sign of coming riches.

If a rooster crows at your window, it is a sign of death.

If a rooster crows on your front or back porch, a stranger is coming.

It is a sign of company if your nostril itches.

If a spider swings down on a web, company is coming.

If you drop a dish cloth, it is a sign of bad luck.

If the crown of your head itches, you will soon be advanced to a more honorable position.

If your right eye jumps, it is a sign of bad luck.

If your left eye jumps, it is a sign of money.

If you stub your right toe, it's good luck. If the left toe, then you had better watch out.

If your right foot itches, you are going to walk on strange land.

If a woman enters your house first on Monday morning, it's bad luck.

If a person has never seen his father, he can blow his breath into a baby's mouth and cure the hives.

If a stray cat or dog comes to your house, the household will have good luck.

If a black cat crosses the road at night, you will have bad luck on down the road.

If your foot itches under the bottom, you're going to walk on fresh graveyard dirt or on strange land.

When a dog stretches, he is measuring his grave.

If your nose itches, someone will visit you.

If you see a red bird, a stranger will come to your house.

If a person with black gums bites you, your teeth will fall out.

If your right hand itches, you will get some money. If your left hand itches too, you will get some more money.

If your nose burns, someone is talking about you.

A blister on your tongue means that you have told a lie.

When you have cold shivers, someone is talking about you.

A dogwood tree will live the length of its planter.

If a bird gets in your hair, you will have headaches.

If the sun shines when it is raining, the devil is beating his wife.

The seventh child in every family will be lucky.

If the coach wears a red shirt on the day of the game— good luck.

If the other team's coaches wear plaid shirts on the day of the game—good luck.

The first team on the field will usually lose.

An itching of the lips means that someone is slandering you.

Nose bleeding is a sign of bad luck.

If your left foot itches, you will take an unfortunate journey.

If your stomach itches, you will be invited to a feast.

It is a sign of death for a dog to howl.

A dream of marriage is a sign of death.

To dream of death is a sign of marriage.

To see silver money in your dream is the sign of trouble.

Sudden or shooting pains in the body are signs of bad news.

If bees settle in a house, it is a sure sign of fire or other disasters.

If furniture falls off the load while you are moving, expect sickness or loss.

If the New Year comes in on a dark night, then more Negroes than whites will die, and vice versa.

If you have a piece of money on New Year's, you will have money all year.

To dream of a possum is a sign of hearing of death.

Dream of fish—someone close is expecting a child.

Dream of corn—if the ear is full, wealth is on the way.

When you have nightmare, the witches are riding you.

When you dream about snakes, you have an enemy.

It is a sign of disappointment to brush or comb the hair after dark.

A dark person coming into the house on the beginning of a new year is a sign of bad luck.

If a dove coos at night, someone in the neighborhood will die.

If a dog howls at night, then death will come in its owner's family.

If a writing spider writes your name, you will die.

Rain on the day of burial means the person will go to heaven.

If an owl hoots near the home of a sick person, death is near.

If an owl comes to your window, or you hear him in a tree, someone in your family will die.

If a good man visits your house first on New Year's, you will have good luck, but if a bad man visits your house first you will have bad luck.

Charms

If you sing before making bread, you will cry before it is eaten.

If you sing before breakfast, you will cry before dinner.

If you go to bed without cleaning the table, the youngest in the family will not sleep well.

If you put on your right shoe first, you will be fortunate all day.

If you put your left shoe on first, you will find everything to the contrary.

Never tell a dream until you have broken your fast.

If you sweep someone's feet, he will run off.

If you cross a broom or stick, always step over it backwards to prevent bad luck.

If someone strikes you with a broom, it will cause you to stop growing.

If someone strikes you with a broom, you will never get married.

If you mop or sweep under a sick person's bed, he will die.

Never break eggs on people's front porch, because it will bring disease to the household.

If you ever borrow salt from someone, never return it because you will have bad luck.

Never do any sewing on Ascension Day. If you sew on Ascension Day, lightning will surely strike you.

If you break a mirror, don't sweep it up for seven hours. If you do, you will have hard bad luck for seven weeks afterwards.

Put a wishbone up over the door, and the first man that enters is the man you will marry.

If two people comb your hair, the youngest will die.

If you catch a butterfly, you will get a dress the same color.

If your dress hem turns up, kiss it and you will get a new dress.

If you bite off the head of a yellow butterfly, you will get a new dress.

Never wear red to a funeral; vou will be the next one to die.

Never look back at a funeral procession; you will be the next to die.

Never walk over graves—you will die.

If a woman wears her husband's clothes, he will have bad luck.

Don't twirl a chair on one leg; you are turning friends from you.

It is bad luck to destroy spiders.

If you forget something, never go back home for it or you will have bad luck.

It is bad luck for two persons to look in a mirror at the same time.

You will have bad luck if you leave a sealed letter in the house overnight.

Always go out of the same door you go in, if you have never been to that place before, to prevent bad luck.

It is very unlucky to remove a long-worn ring from the finger.

It is unlucky to pick up an old glove.

It is unlucky for a maiden to marry in colors or a widow to marry in white.

It is bad to postpone marriage.

Dancing is not a sin unless you cross your legs while dancing.

It's bad luck to give your sweetheart a gift with a sharp point.

Never sweep a pin out of the door, because it will cut your good luck off.

Girls should never climb an apple tree, because the tree will die.

A horseshoe over the door keeps out evil spirits .

If two people say the same thing simultaneously, one should knock on wood; if not, bad luck will come to one.

Never burn two lights in one room; you will have bad luck.

If you spill salt, you will have bad luck.

May is an unlucky month to marry in.

If a task is started on a Friday and not finished, it will take a long time to finish it.

Never move on Saturday.

When you move, take all your furniture at one time. It is bad luck to go back for the second time; you will not stay long in your new home.

Never go back in the same house or room after you have moved.

Don't sit on a trunk if you are going someplace. If you do, you will be disappointed.

It's bad luck to move into a house with an old broom.

Never enter a house that you are moving in for the first time without a box of table salt.

Burning old shoes will cause all snakes to leave the area.

The event of death in the family can be made known to the bees by jingling keys or beating a small pan; otherwise another death will occur within a year.

When passing a graveyard, always cross your fingers; if you don't, you will die.

Never wash on New Year's; someone in your family will die.

If you watch a hearse out of sight, your mother will die.

If the sign of the zodiac is in the head and you have a tooth pulled, you will die. [The luck is the same for any kind of operation. All things must be done according to the sign.]

Never sweep dirt out of the house after dark, because someone in your family will die the next week.

If you're walking with someone and stomp your toe, turn around and pat the other fellow on the back. If you don't, your whole toe may decay.

If you point at a graveyard, you better bite your finger as hard as you can, or else it will decay.

Never plant a cedar tree. If the tree dies, you will die.

If you stump your left toe, turn around three times to ward off bad luck.

If a sick person hits you, hit him back; if not, you will die when he does.

Never eat fish and ice cream together; it will kill you.

If a woman cuts her hair, she will be weak.

If a bird builds a nest and uses one hair from your head, you will have a headache for six months.

If you forget about a wart on the body, it will leave.

If you count your warts, make a knot in a thread for every wart, and throw the thread away, the wart will be cured.

If an old person points his finger at you, whatever he says about you or to you will come true.

If you show the new moon a new piece of money, you will get more money, providing you see it clearly.

If you wash your hair in the first May rain, your hair will grow.

If you wear a blacksnake hide around your waist, you can whip any man in the world.

If you eat collard greens, hog jowls, black-eyed peas, and corn bread on New Year's Day, you will have good luck all year.

If a black cat crosses in front of you and you do not spit three times and turn around three times, you will have bad luck.

If you go to the cemetery at twelve midnight when the moon is full, you can see the dead walking around.

Never take the ashes out after the sun sets or before the sun comes up.

Put a knife or spoon under the mattress to prevent nightmares.

If your hair is caught in a running brook, you will have a running mind.

If two people sit in the same chair, one of them will die.

If you hang an adder's skin in the rafters, your house will never catch fire.

If you place a broomstick under a cooking pan you can hear the devil beating his wife.

If you have a tooth pulled, place it under your pillow and it will turn to money.

If your enemy places his hand on your head, all of your hair will fall out.

To take up ashes between Christmas and New Year's—bad luck.

Never borrow onions or garlic—bad luck.

It's bad luck to put your hat on the bed.

It's bad luck to open an umbrella in the house.

It's bad luck to wear two hats.

It's bad luck to put on another's hat, unless you blow your breath in it three times.

Never go out of the front door and come right back in the back door, because it will cut your company off.

Never kill a toadfrog. Warts will develop over your body.

Never walk directly in someone's footsteps—you will have bad luck.

Killing a spider is bad luck.

If you count the number of fish you have caught, you will catch no more that day.

If the players eat peanuts before a game, it will cause bad luck.

A hair cut before a game will make you weak, causing your team to lose the game.

To take a full bath on the day of the game—bad luck.

If players eat anything other than soup—bad luck.

It is bad luck to pass a sharp instrument to another.

If you step over a fishing pole, you will have bad luck.

You will never have good luck if you grow an ivy plant in your house.

If you are touched or hit with a broom, always spit on it or you will go to jail.

Don't let a black cat cross your trail going to the left; you will have bad luck. But if he goes to the right, you will have good luck.

Never sleep with your shoes under the bed.

Never look at a cross-eyed person.

If you look at an undressed woman, you will lose your money.

Never sweep dust out of your house after sundown, because you are sweeping someone out of your family.

4

Folk Rhymes and Verse

When you get married and live down south,
don't forget me and my big mouth.

Rhythm is one of the most pervasive aspects of the heritage that the American Negro has received from his African ancestors. Whether in the form of feet dancing to a rhythmic beat, or pungent and suggestive rhymed couplets, quatrains, or other verse forms, the creations resulting from this inheritance are significant contributions to American culture.

Some of the best Negro folk verse is in children's rhymes that comment on specific incidents or individuals; others express emotional reactions and taunt friends in a cordial and congenial manner. This latter genre is called the·"Autograph Album Rhyme" and is written in students' autograph booklets at the close of the school year, along with the writer's name and address. This practice has been in existence for a number of years and is still indulged in by high school students. Strangely enough, some of the rhymes used as far back as sixty years ago are still being quoted; others are of recent invention; and others are coined daily.

Negro adult verse has not flourished in North Carolina as have children's rhymes, nor can it be said to conform to any fixed pattern or theme. Rarely, if ever, does one find as many as three or four adult productions fitting a common pattern.

North Carolina Negro adult rhymes are few and far between, and on widely scattered subjects, ranging from verse about animals to narratives of high-life and low-life characters and their comments on specific incidents.

Most of the North Carolina Negro adult group's versification deals with individual feelings, experiences, or personal opinions about life and its manifold ramifications. It is interesting to note that tales about 'Bre'r Rabbit,' and other animal tales, once widely told, have practically disappeared from the Negro's living tradition in North Carolina, but that one of the favorite group-property verses invented by the North Carolina Negro today is the narrative in which the monkey is the central figure.

Children's Autograph Album Rhymes

You are sharp as a tack, never dull;
Just like a peanut in a hull.

Beauty is only skin deep and ugly is to the bone;
Beauty fades away, but ugly hangs on.

Love all, trust few;
Learn to paddle your own canoe.

Sitting still fishing makes no one great.
The good Lord sends the fishes, you must dig the bait.

Blue is a color, red is too;
Try a smile when you feel blue.

Remember the M, remember the E;
Put them together and remember ME.

Corns really hurt, they give you the blues;
Remember that fact and buy fitting shoes.

When you marry and get out of shape,
Get you a girdle for $2.98.

The Mississippi River is deep and wide;
Catch a alligator to the other side.

Girls are made of sugar and spice;
Boys aren't made, they just shoot dice.

Green is green, red is red;
Study each day! Put knowledge in your head!

The moon is in the sky, and so is the sun;
Study first, then have your fun.

When you get old and think you're sweet,
Take off your shoes, and smell your feet.

When you're at a party and they drink alcohol,
Remember it's not needed to have you a ball.

I wish you luck, I wish you joy,
I wish you first a baby boy;
And when his hair begins to curl,
I wish you next a baby girl;
And when her hair begins to knot,
I guess you know it's time to stop.

When in the line of business,
And you don't have a business of your own,
Make it your business
To leave other peoples' alone.

Be humble enough to always obey;
You will be giving orders yourself some day.

Before you can get the rabbit out of the log,
You will have to learn to bark like a dog.

I've told you once; I've told you twice;
Don't be a mother before you're a wife.

Sugar is white, butter is yellow;
I think you will make a very nice fellow!

Up on the mountain, shining like tin;
The way I love you, baby, it's a doggone sin.

Pigs like mud, cows like squash;
I like you, I do, by gosh.

Needles and pins, needles and pins;
When I met you, my life beginned.

The boys think I'm sweet, the girls think I'm kind.
I would like to know what's on your mind.

I'm writing you this letter, darling, I would write it in gold;
But ink is all my pen will hold.

Ice cream city, candy state,
This sweet letter don't need no date.

Up on a house top, baking a cake,
The way I love you is no mistake.

I don't make love by the garden gate,
For love is blind, but the neighbors ain't.

If you want your man, better keep him by your side;
If he flags my train, I'm sure gonna let him ride.

The higher the mountain, the cooler the breeze,
The lighter the couple, the harder they squeeze.

I've got a cute little shape, and a pretty little figure;
Stand back, big boys, until I get a little bigger!

I love you once, I love you twice;
Baby, I love you next to Jesus Christ.

When your heart tells you you're in a rut,
Tell your heart to keep its big mouth shut.

Milk is milk, cheese is cheese;
What is a kiss without a squeeze?

Choice kind of fish don't bite any kind of line;
You have to go deep-sea fishing to find my kind.

When you marry, marry good;
Make your husband cut your wood!

You're my morning milk, my evening cream,
My all-day study, and my midnight dream.

Roses on my shoulders, slippers on my feet;
I'm my mother's baby, don't you think I'm sweet?

Apples on the shelf, peaches in the bowl,
Can't get a sweetheart to save my soul.

Up on the mountain, five feet high,
I love you, baby, that ain't no lie.

A bulldog barked in London,
A German shepherd barked in Spain,

But the love I got for you, baby,
Would make any dog break his chain.

I love you, I love you, I love you so well,
If I had a peanut, I'd give you the shell.

Columbus's best discovery was in 1492,
But my best discovery was when I met you.

Pork chops, veal chops, make a little gravy;
I love you baby, and I don't mean maybe.

Sugar is sugar, salt is salt;
The way I love you, it ain't my fault.

Orange city, lemon state;
Squeeze me dear, I forgot the date.

You never miss your water till your well runs dry,
You never miss your baby till he says goodbye.

Rocks got the mountain, fishes got the sea,
Loves got you, baby, and troubles got me.

As green grass grows around the stump,
I want you for my darling sugar lump.

Huckle buck city, be-bopin' state,
A letter like this don't need no date.

Up on the house top, ten feet high,
If you don't love me, I hope to die.

I'd rather be in Poland, playing in the sand,
Than to see some other woman messing with my man.

The river is wide, and I can't step it;
I love you baby, and I just can't help it.

A boy is like a dip of snuff—
Take one dip and that's enough.

When you get married, and live in a wagon,
The bottom falls out, but your feet keeps draggin'.

If a man makes a mistake, the world forgives;
A woman has to suffer as long as she lives.

When you get married and your husband gets cross,
Get you a broom and show him who's boss.

When you get married and have nineteen,
Don't call it a family, but call it a baseball team.

When you get married and have twenty-four,
Don't stop there, the Army needs lots more.

When you get married and your husband gets drunk,
Put him in the trunk and sell him for junk.

When you get married and have twenty-five,
Don't call it a family, call it a tribe!

The river is wide, the boat is floating,
Darling, let's marry and stop this courting!

Ice is ice, rice is rice;
One day, baby, you'll be my wife.

Apples on the table, peaches on the shelf,
Baby, I'm getting tired of sleeping by myself.

When you get married and live in China,
Remember me back in old North Carolina.

Life is sweet, life is swell,
But when you marry, life is hell.

When you marry and live across the lake,
Send me a kiss by a rattlesnake.

When you get married and live upstairs,
Don't fall down putting on airs.

When you marry don't marry a cook,
Marry a man with a fat pocketbook.

When you marry and live across the sea,
Send me a cocoanut C.O.D.

Lions in the cage, monkeys in the zoo,
Who wants to marry a fool like you?

If you don't like my apples, don't shake my tree;
I ain't after your man, he's after me.

When you get married and live out west,
I'll send your mail by the Jigger express.

Adults' Rhymes and Songs

Strawberry pie and huckleberry puddin',
I'd give it all way for de love of Sally Goodin'.

Six cents cotton and forty cents meat,
How in de worl' can a po' man eat?

I'm gonna starve like everybody will,
'Cause I can't make a livin' at de cotton mill.

Down behin' de henhouse on my knees,
I thought I heard a chicken sneeze;
It was only de rooster saying his prayers,
Singin' out hymns to all de hens upstairs.

Oh Cap'n! Oh Cap'n! my feet am col';
Cap'n say, "Damn yo' feet, let de wheelbarrow roll."

Light on de handle, heavy on de steel,
De hotter de sunshine, de better I feel.

Thank God and bless the food;
Damn the Devil—let him wash the dishes.

THE POOL-SHOOTING MONKEY

Down in the jungle where the trees grow tall,
There's a pool-shootin' monkey talkin' junk to 'em all.
Everybody could tell he was a real big score,
They could tell this fact by the clothes he wore.
He wore gabardine pants, with a shirt to match,
And of greenback money, he had a batch.
He wore a pink vest with a polka-dot tie,
If he wasn't sharp, I hope to die.
He wore a gray plaid coat, with a belt in the back,
He drove a great long car called a Cadillac.
Now he dropped in the poolroom and picked up the stick,
And he practiced from three till a quarter to six.
He came back in the poolroom talkin' his jive,
He say, "Who wanna try the baddest guy alive?"
The baboon looked up from the corner of his eyes,
And said, "I'll try you just this one for size."
So the monkey ran the one, two, and spotted the three,
He said, "Watch this while I have a bit of tea."
The monkey came back—ran the three, four, five,
This brought salty tears to the baboon's eyes.
Then the monkey ran the six, seven, eight, nine, and ten,
And the baboon started to cry again.
Then the monkey ran the eleven, twelve, thirteen—and
    fourteen on the side,
And said, "Now do you believe I'm gonna carry this fifteen
    for a hell of a ride?"

THE SIGNIFYING MONKEY

It was early in the morning, and late in May,
When the lion passed down the monkey's way.
Said the monkey to the lion, "There's a great big joker
    down by the bay,
Talkin' 'bout yo' kin in a real bad way.
He said some things I'm afraid to say.
He said yo' pa was awful cheap, that yo' sister's a louse,
And yo' ma talks more'n anybody in the South."
The lion stood up and let out a mighty roar,
And his tail popped out like a forty-fo'.
The lion found the elephant asleep under a tree,
And said, "Get up, big boy, it's gonna be you and me!
What's this I hear 'bout you gonna pin my ears,
And I ain't lost a fight in fifty years?
You talked about my kin the livelong day,
So, before I leave here, you're gonna pay."
The lion swung at the elephant, and the elephant ducked,
From then on in the lion had no luck.
They fought all day, an' they fought all night,
Don't see how the lion got outa that fight.
The elephant messed up his jaw, and messed up his face,
He knocked his nose right outa place.
Yes sir, when that lion drug through the jungle mo' dead
    than alive,
That's when that signifying monkey started his jive.
"Talking 'bout you're the king of the beasts,
Your face looks like it's been et by yeast.
You left here this mornin' on a jungle run,
An' come back this evening, lookin' like you hung.

Oh no, don't you roar,
Cause I'll jump down from here an' beat you some more.
Fu'thermo', ever time I try to git a little res',
Here you come with that ol' roarin' mess.
And don't say that you didn't git beat,
'Cause I was sittin' right here in my ringside seat.
Quit scratchin' on my tree with your sharp big paw,
'Fore I take me a cocoanut an' break yo' jaw.
An' another thing I want you to know,
I been goin' out with your sister for a month or so."
The monkey became so enthused, goin' 'round and 'round,
Till his left foot slipped, and he hit the ground.
Like a ball of lightning and a streak of hcat,
The lion was on him with all four feet.
The monkey begged, "Please, Mr. Lion, I was just lyin',"
But the lion said, "No, I'm gonna stop you from signifyin'."
The monkey said, "Okay, stand back like a man should,
An' I'll fight you all over these bloomin' woods.
Jus' let me git my feet flat on this sand,
An' I'll fight you like a natural man."
So the lion stood back and squared off for a fight,
But the monkey took two hops and was out of sight.

THE BALLAD OF HARRISON NEAL

Set down, frien', an' pour you a dram,
While I sing you a song 'bout a big black man.
Wid a heart of gold an' muscles of steel,
He been knowed far an' wide as Harrison Neal.

He live on de farm till he been nine,
Den he pappy got kilt in de Randolph mine.
Den he mammy say, "Dear Lawd, help me,
Cain't feed my chaps nuttin' but cawnbread, 'lasses, an'
    sassyfras tea."

Neal he say, "Mammy, don' you sell de mule or de cow,
'Cause we gwine to make it anyhow.
Keep dese chaps workin' dis lan',
Make a crop, den I come back an' give you a han.'

"I's gwine down de river where dey buil'in' de dam,
An' get me a job from de corntractin' man.
Save mos' my money an' bring it to you,
Mo' samer dan a good boy ought to do."

So Neal he set out 'fo' de break of day,
Dark an' stormy wid de lightnin' showin' him de way.
He reach de river 'bout seven o'clock,
Say, "Gimme a job drillin' dis rock."

Straw boss say, "Mister Ben been gone,
Got a full crew, can't put you on.
But, boy, I kind of likes yo' spunk,
So I make you water boy, if you don' get drunk."

So Neal say, "Yassuh, I's been dat befo',
I knows how de water-totin' racket go."
So he grabs up some buckets an' runs like hell,
An' brings de men's water from de company well.

He do his job good, an' he make de day,
An' hold on fast till he get his pay.
Den' when de rock pile ain't no mo',
He goes back home an' knocks on de do'.

Say, "Mama, dis heah's yo' gone-son Neal,
What come back to help you in de 'bacco fiel'.
I's got lots of money in my pockets, too,
Dat I done brung home to de chaps and you."

So his mammy grab Neal an' she hug him tight,
Say, "Neal, I knowed you'd turn out right.
Come on in, boy, an' rest yo'self,
While I fetches some ham offen' de smokehouse shelf."

From dat day on, for many a year,
Neal stayed home, didn't go nowhere.
Stayed right dere till time run by;
An his po' old mammy laid down an' die.

JACK JOHNSON AND JIM JEFFRIES

Amaze an' Grace, how sweet it sounds,
Jack Johnson knocked Jim Jeffries down.
Jim Jeffries jumped up an' hit Jack on the chin,
An' then Jack knocked him down agin.

The Yankees hold the play,
The white man pulls the trigger;
But it make no difference what the white man say,
The world champion's still a nigger.

A COUNTY ROAD SONG

1

I went to jail and they served beans, beans, beans,
I went to jail and they served beans, beans, beans,
Oh they never served lamb, chicken, or ham,
I'm sho' gettin' tired of eatin' beans, beans, beans.

CHORUS:
I'm gettin' tired of eatin' beans, beans, beans,
I'm 'gettin' tired of eatin' beans, beans, beans.

2

They sent me to the road and I ate beans, beans, beans,
They sent me to the road and I ate beans, beans, beans,
Oh they never served lamb, chicken, or ham,
I'm sho' gettin' tired of eatin' beans, beans, beans.

3

I went home and my wife served beans, beans, beans,
I went home and my wife served beans, beans, beans,
She never served lamb, chicken, or ham,
I'm sho' gittin' tired of eatin' beans, beans, beans.

YOU-ALL

Come all of you from other parts,
Both city folks and rural,
And listen while I tell you this,
The word "you-all" is plural!
When we say, "You-all come down,"
Or, "We-all shall be lonely,"
We mean a dozen folks, perhaps,
And not one person only.
If I should say to Rastus Jones,
For instance, "You-all's lazy,"
Or, "Will you-all lend me your knife?"
He'd think that I was crazy.
Now, if you'd be more sociable,
And with us often mingle,
You'd find that on the native tongue,
You-all is never single.
Don't think I mean to criticize,
Or act as if I knew all,
But when we speak of one alone,
We all say, "I like you-all."

A TOAST

I do believe that the Good Lord above,
Put you on earth just for poor me to love.
So I picked you out from all the rest,
Because you know, DARLING, I love you best.
I once had a heart, and it was true,
But now it's gone from me to you.
So take care of my heart as I have done,
'Cause you have two hearts now, and I have none.
And if I go to Heaven, and you're not there,
I'll write your name on the golden stair.
And if you're not there by Judgment Day,
I'll know you went the other way.
But just to show you, DEAR, that my love is true,
I'd go to hell to be with you.

THE SAINTLY MAN

Sometimes, Old Pal, in the morning,
When the dawn is cold and grey,
I lie in the perfumed feathers,
Thinking thoughts that I'd dare not say.
Then I look at the morning paper,
And see where some saintly man,
Who had never been slapped in all his life,
Or never said hell or damn,
Who had never been out till the wee hours,
Or jotted a gay soubrette,
But who preached on the evils of drinking,
Of cards, and of cigarettes,
Was cut off in the prime of a useful life,
The headlines glibly say,
Or snatched by the dark grim reaper,
He's done crossed the Great Highway.
They buried him deep—a few friends will weep,
But the world will move on with a sigh.
And the saintly man will soon be forgot,
The same as you and I.

LUCY JACKSON *

Lucy Jackson was a pretty yellow gal,
She never went to church at all.
But when de circus came to town one day,
She met de preacher out in de hall,
And said, "Brother Parson, hold me tight,
For as sho' as I been born,
I knows by de way I's feelin',
I feels religion comin' on."

* An old-time minstrel song, as sung in the "Rabbit Foot" show, and the "Florida Blossoms" minstrel show, in the early 1900's.

Songs used by Negro college students in sit-in, stand-in, and kneel-in demonstrations.

WE SHALL NOT BE MOVED

We shall not, we shall not be moved,
We shall not, we shall not be moved.
Just like the tree planted by the water,
We shall not be moved.
We're on our way to victory,
We shall not be moved.
We're on our way to victory,
We shall not be moved.
Just like the tree planted by the water,
We shall not be moved.
Come on and join us,
We shall not be moved.
Come on and join us,
We shall not be moved.
Just like the tree planted by the water,
We shall not be moved.

GIVE ME THAT OLD FREEDOM SPIRIT

(Sing to the tune of "That Old-Time Religion")

Give me that old freedom spirit,
Give me that old freedom spirit,
Give me that old freedom spirit,
It's good enough for me.
Oh, give me that O—O—O—
Old freedom spirit,
It's good enough for me.

It was good for Martin King,
It was good for Martin King,
It was good for Martin King,
It's good enough for me.
Oh, give me that O—O—O—
Old freedom spirit,
It's good enough for me.

It was good for our morale,
It was good for our morale,
It was good for our morale,
It was good enough for me.
Oh, give me that O—O—O—
Old freedom spirit,
It's good enough for me.

WE SHALL OVERCOME

We shall overcome,
We shall overcome,
We shall overcome someday.
Deep in my heart, I do believe,
We shall overcome some day.

Jim Crow cannot last,
Jim Crow cannot last,
Jim Crow cannot last always.
Deep in my heart, I do believe,
Jim Crow cannot last always.

We will be all right,
We will be all right,
We will be all right someday.
Deep in my heart, I do believe,
We will be all right some day.

WE SHALL BE FREE

We shall be free,
We shall be free,
Deep in our hearts, we are not afraid,
We shall be free some day.
As sure as we are
Backed by the NAACP,
We shall be free some day.
We shall be free,
Times may be hard, but we still trust the Lord,
We shall be free some day.
Deep in our hearts,
We are not afraid,
We shall be free some day.

Index

(Folktales and Anecdotes are in roman type. Folk Rhymes and Songs are in *italics*.)